THE LEGEND OF KORRA

Created by
BRYAN KONIETZKO
MICHAEL DANTE DiMARTINO

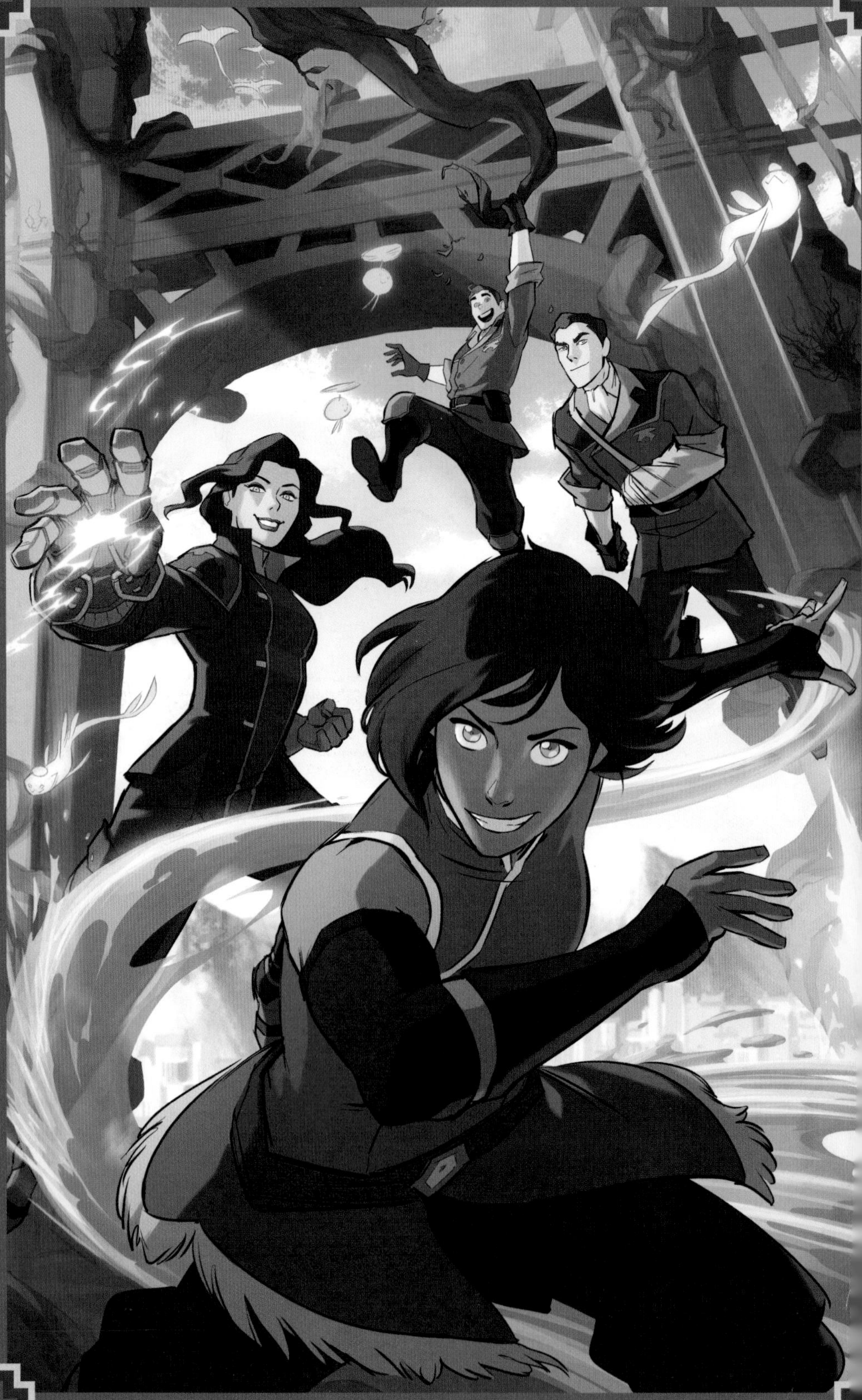

THE LEGEND OF KORRA

TURF WARS · PART ONE

written by
MICHAEL DANTE DiMARTINO

art by
IRENE KOH

colors by
KILLIAN NG

lettering by
NATE PIEKOS of Blambot®

cover by
HEATHER CAMPBELL with **JANE BAK**

DARK HORSE BOOKS

president and publisher **MIKE RICHARDSON**

editor **DAVE MARSHALL**   assistant editor **RACHEL ROBERTS**

designer **SARAH TERRY**   digital art technician **CHRISTIANNE GOUDREAU**

Special thanks to Linda Lee, Kat van Dam, James Salerno, and Joan Hilty
at Nickelodeon, and to Bryan Konietzko and Michael Dante DiMartino.

Published by **DARK HORSE BOOKS**
A division of Dark Horse Comics LLC
10956 SE Main Street, Milwaukie, OR 97222

DARKHORSE.COM | **NICK.COM**

To find a comic shop in your area, visit comicshoplocator.com

First edition: July 2017 | ISBN 978-1-50670-015-1

5 7 9 10 8 6
Printed in the United States of America

Neil Hankerson Executive Vice President • Tom Weddle Chief Financial Officer • Randy Stradley Vice
President of Publishing • Nick McWhorter Chief Business Development Officer • Dale LaFountain Chief
Information Officer • Matt Parkinson Vice President of Marketing • Vanessa Todd-Holmes Vice President
of Production and Scheduling • Mark Bernardi Vice President of Book Trade and Digital Sales • Ken
Lizzi General Counsel • Dave Marshall Editor in Chief • Davey Estrada Editorial Director • Chris Warner
Senior Books Editor • Cary Grazzini Director of Specialty Projects • Lia Ribacchi Art Director • Matt
Dryer Director of Digital Art and Prepress • Michael Gombos Senior Director of Licensed Publications •
Kari Yadro Director of Custom Programs • Kari Torson Director of International Licensing • Sean Brice
Director of Trade Sales

Library of Congress Cataloging-in-Publication Data

Names: DiMartino, Michael Dante, author. | Koh, Irene (Comic book artist),
  artist. | Ng, Killian, colourist. | Piekos, Nate, letterer.
Title: The Legend of Korra : turf wars / written by Michael Dante DiMartino ;
  art by Irene Koh.
Other titles: Legend of Korra (Television program)
Description: First edition. | Milwaukie, OR : Dark Horse Books, 2017- | Part
  one: colors by Killian Ng ; lettering by Nate Piekos of Blambot ; cover by
  Heather Campbell with Jane Bak.
Identifiers: LCCN 2017015317 | ISBN 9781506700151 (part one : paperback)
Subjects: LCSH: Comic books, strips, etc. | BISAC: COMICS & GRAPHIC NOVELS /
  Media Tie-In.
Classification: LCC PN6728.L434 D56 2017 | DDC 741.5/973--dc23
LC record available at https://lccn.loc.gov/2017015317

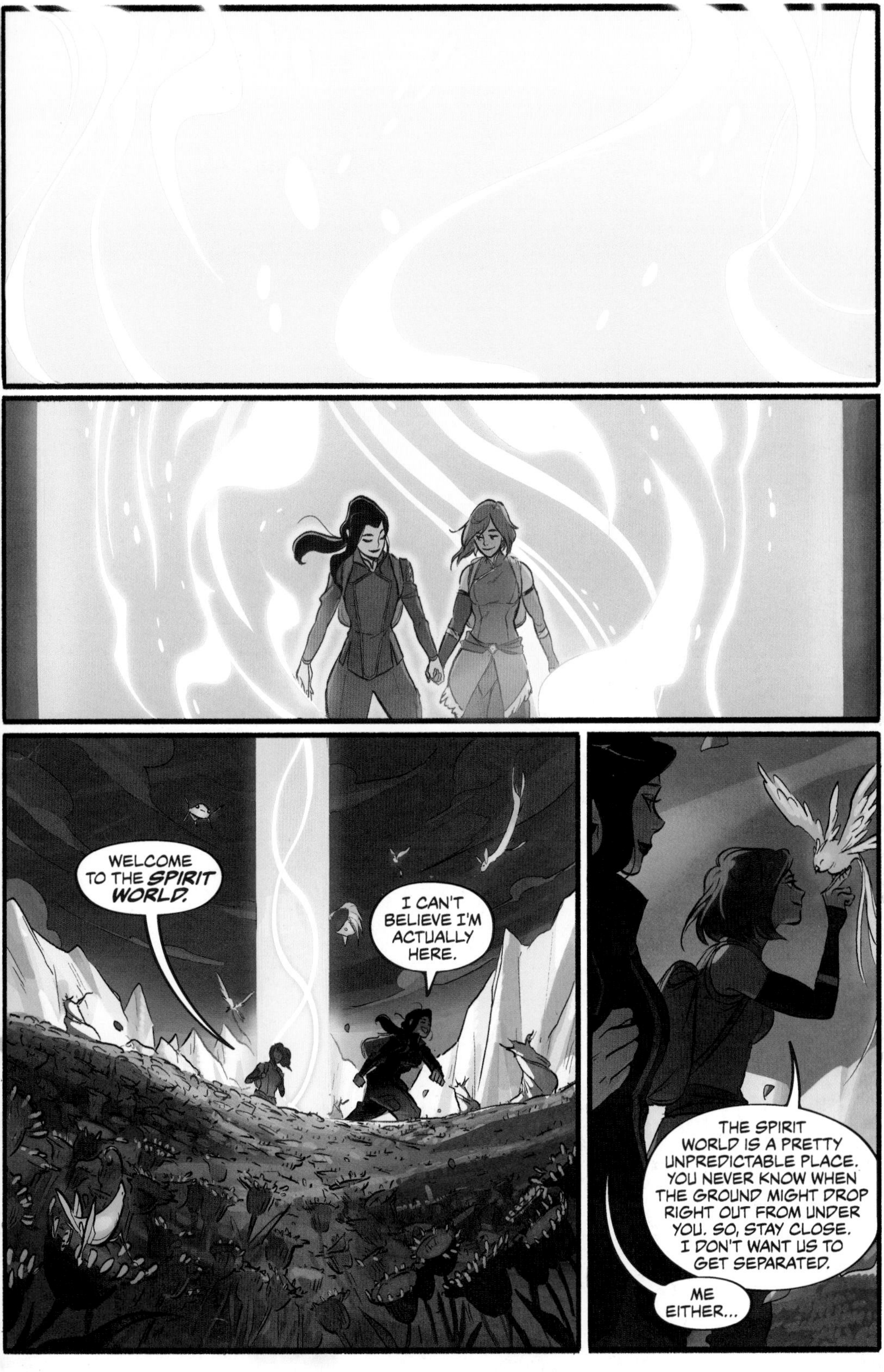
WELCOME TO THE SPIRIT WORLD.
I CAN'T BELIEVE I'M ACTUALLY HERE.
THE SPIRIT WORLD IS A PRETTY UNPREDICTABLE PLACE. YOU NEVER KNOW WHEN THE GROUND MIGHT DROP RIGHT OUT FROM UNDER YOU. SO, STAY CLOSE. I DON'T WANT US TO GET SEPARATED.
ME EITHER...

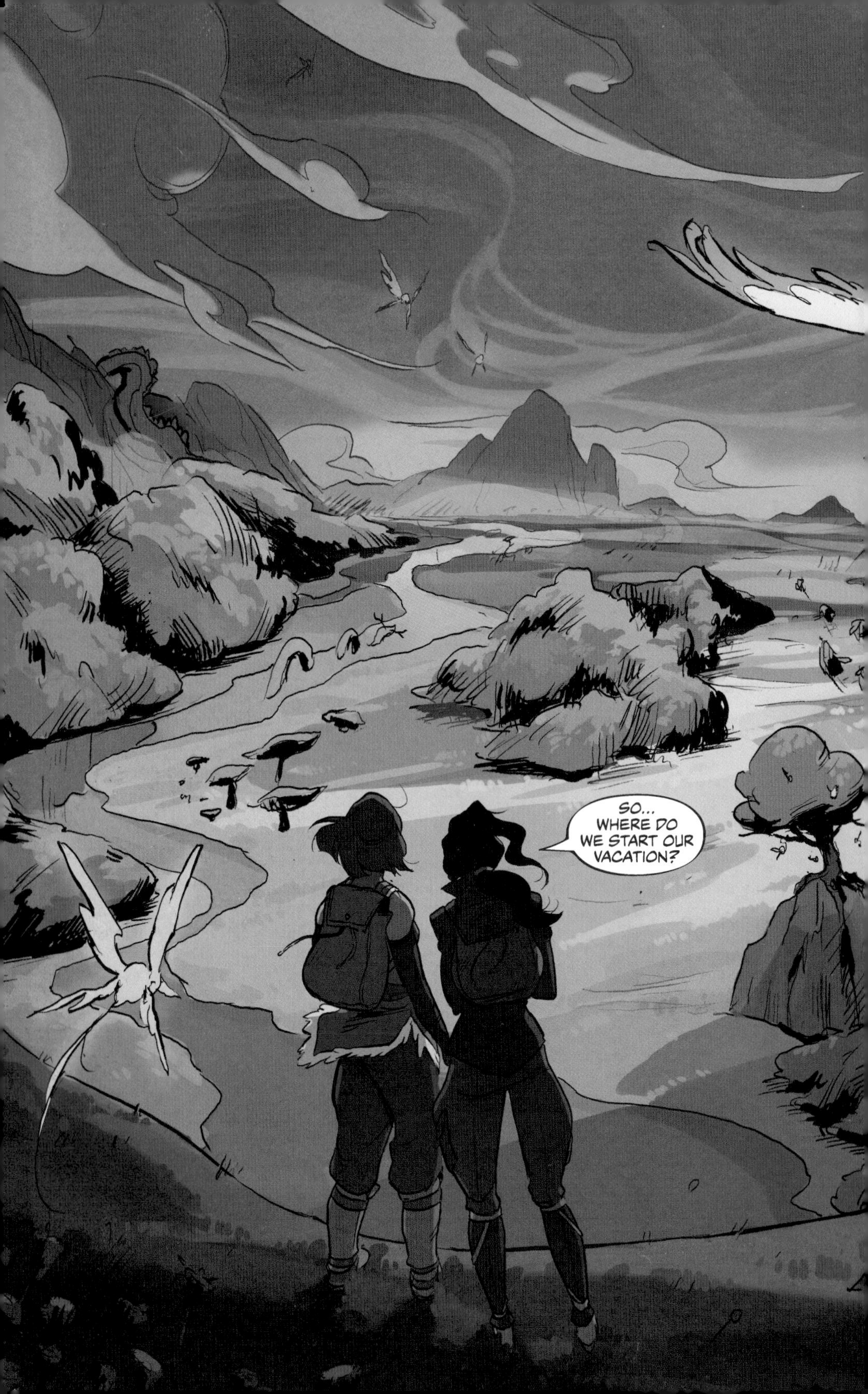
SO... WHERE DO WE START OUR VACATION?

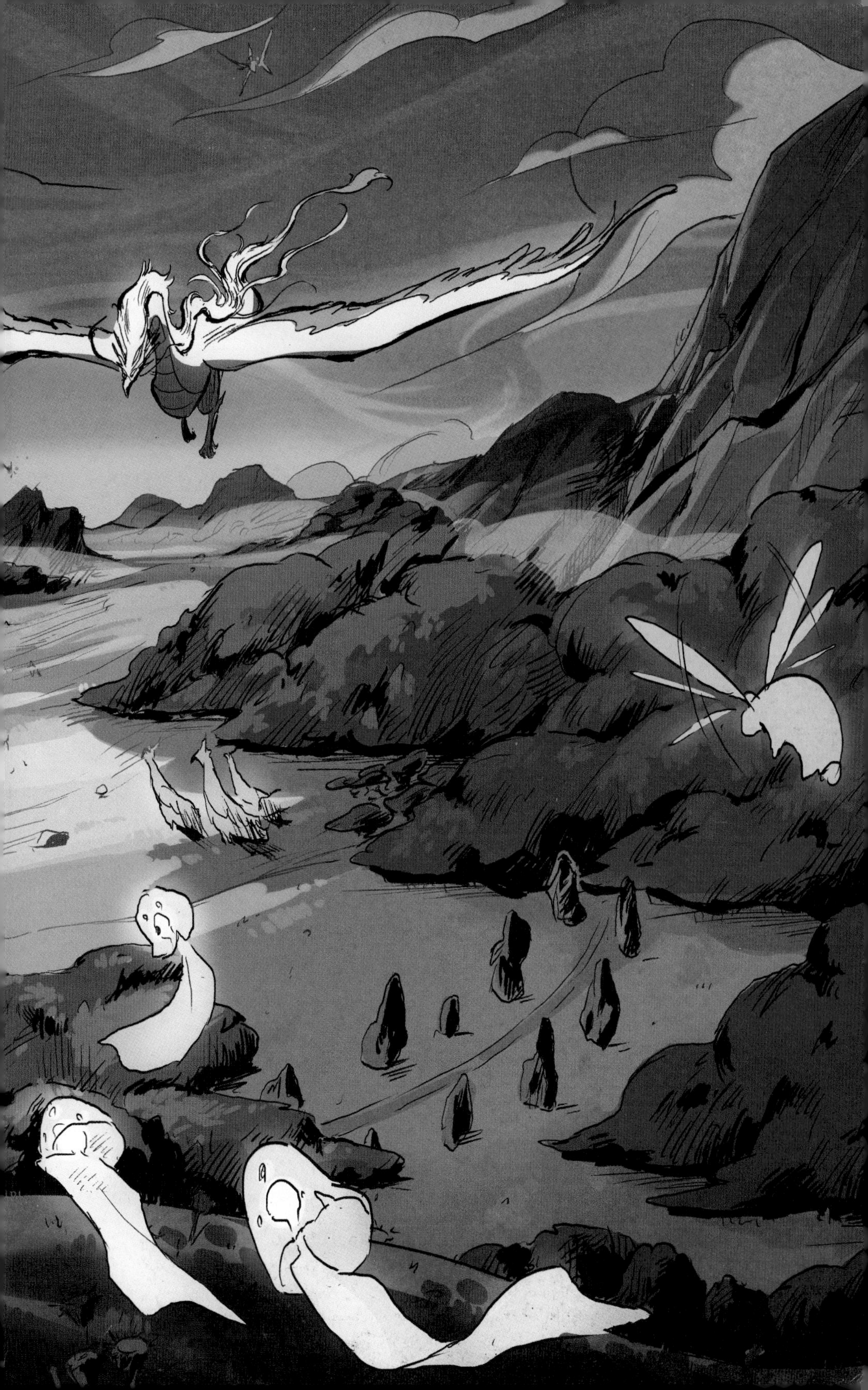

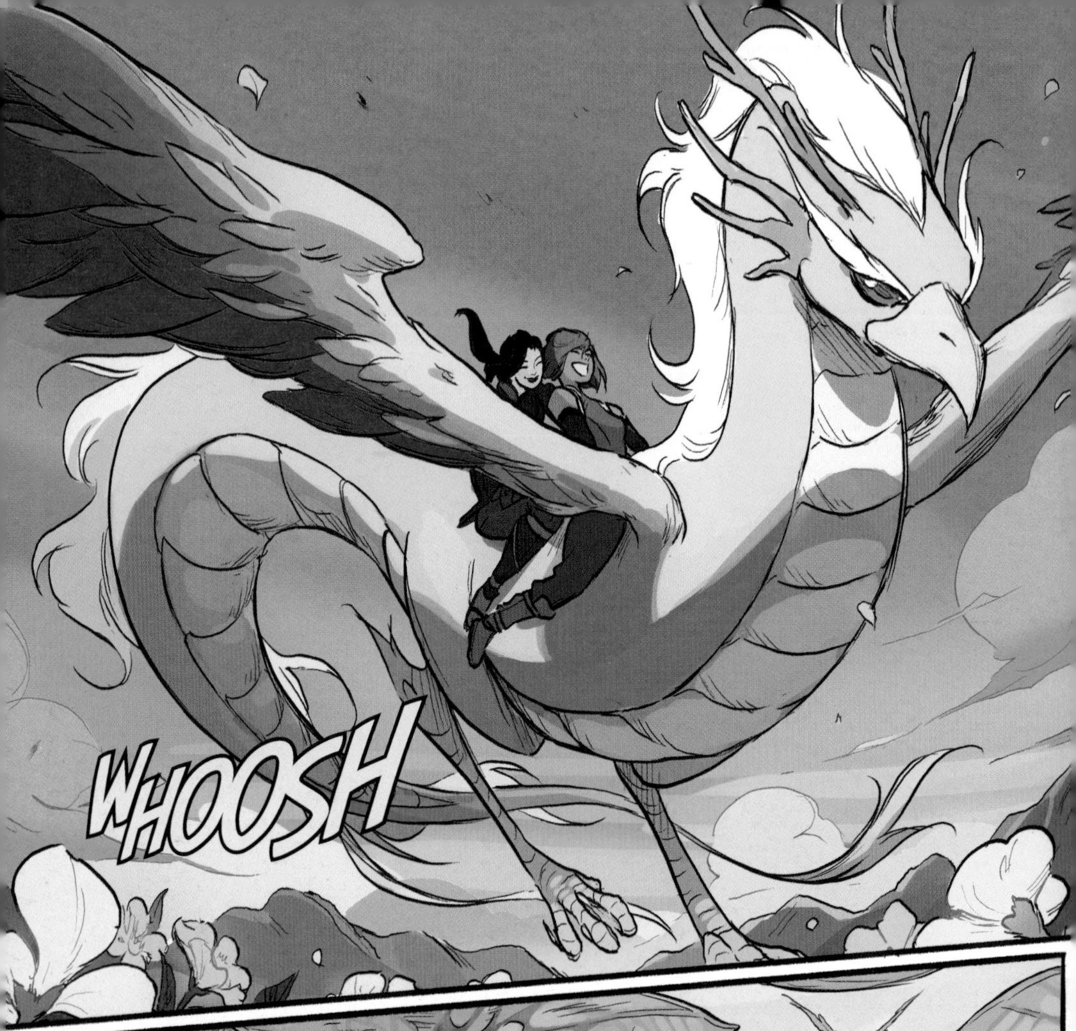
WHOOSH

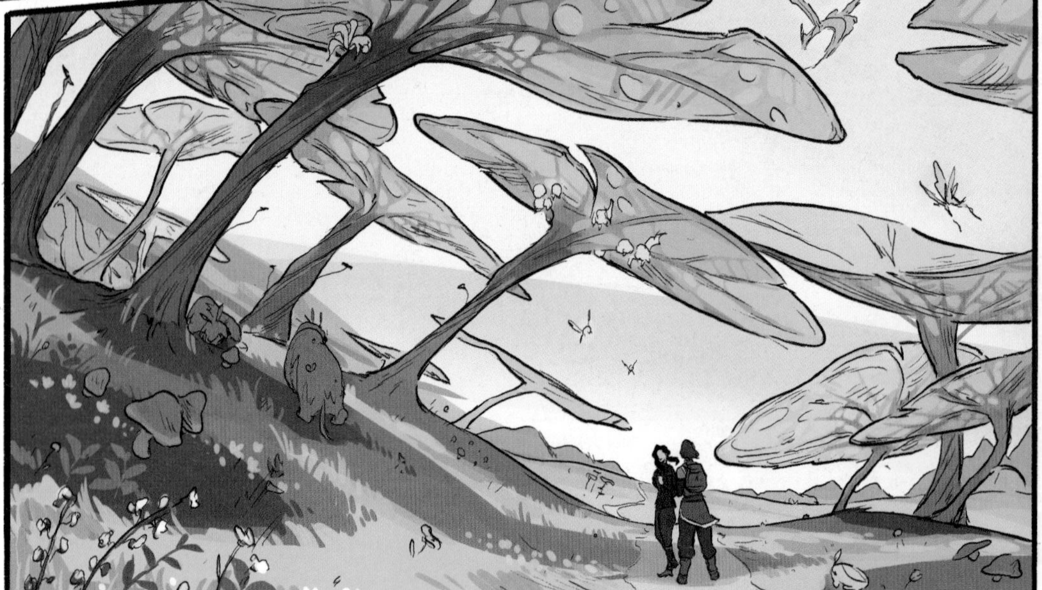

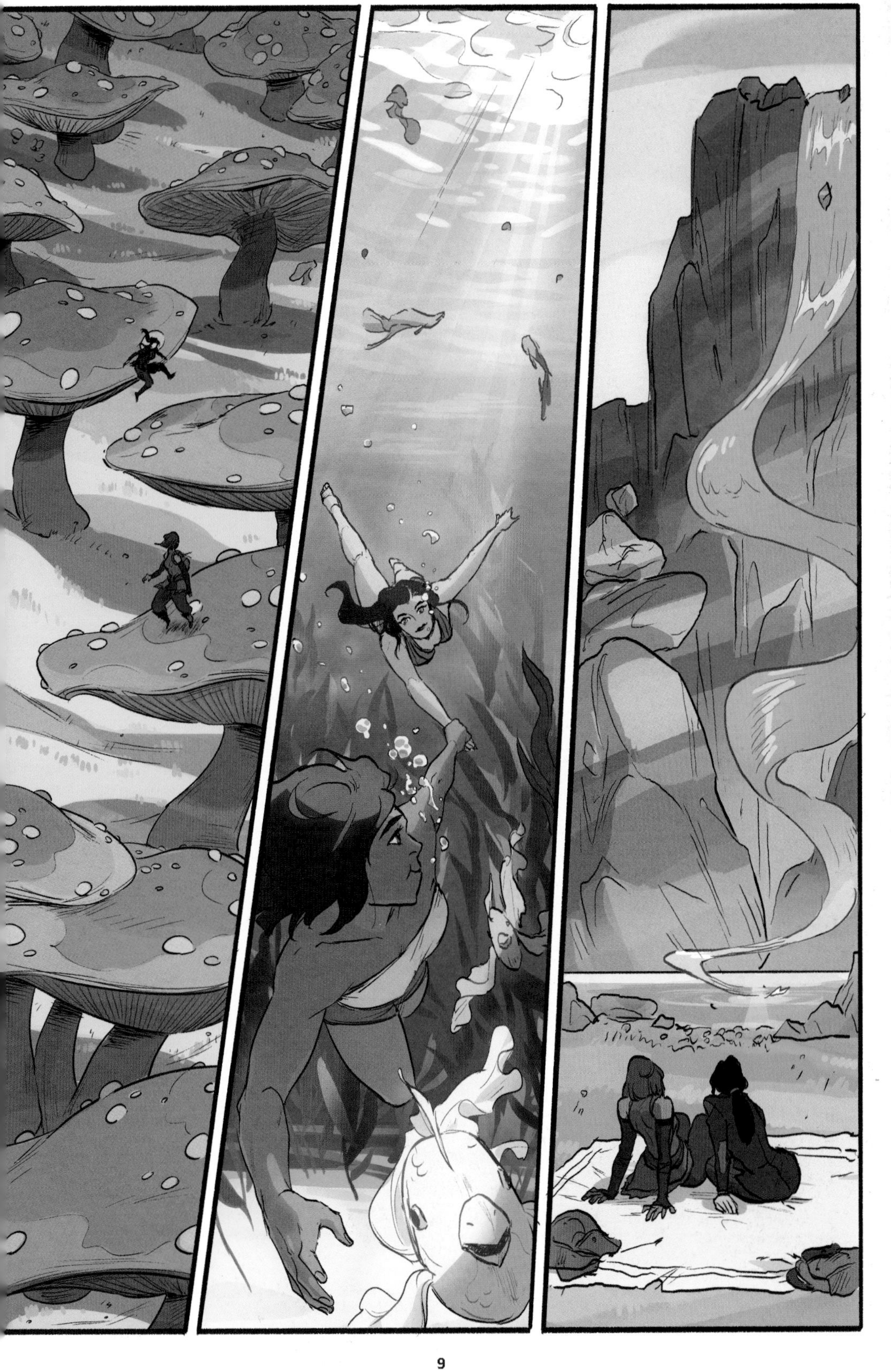

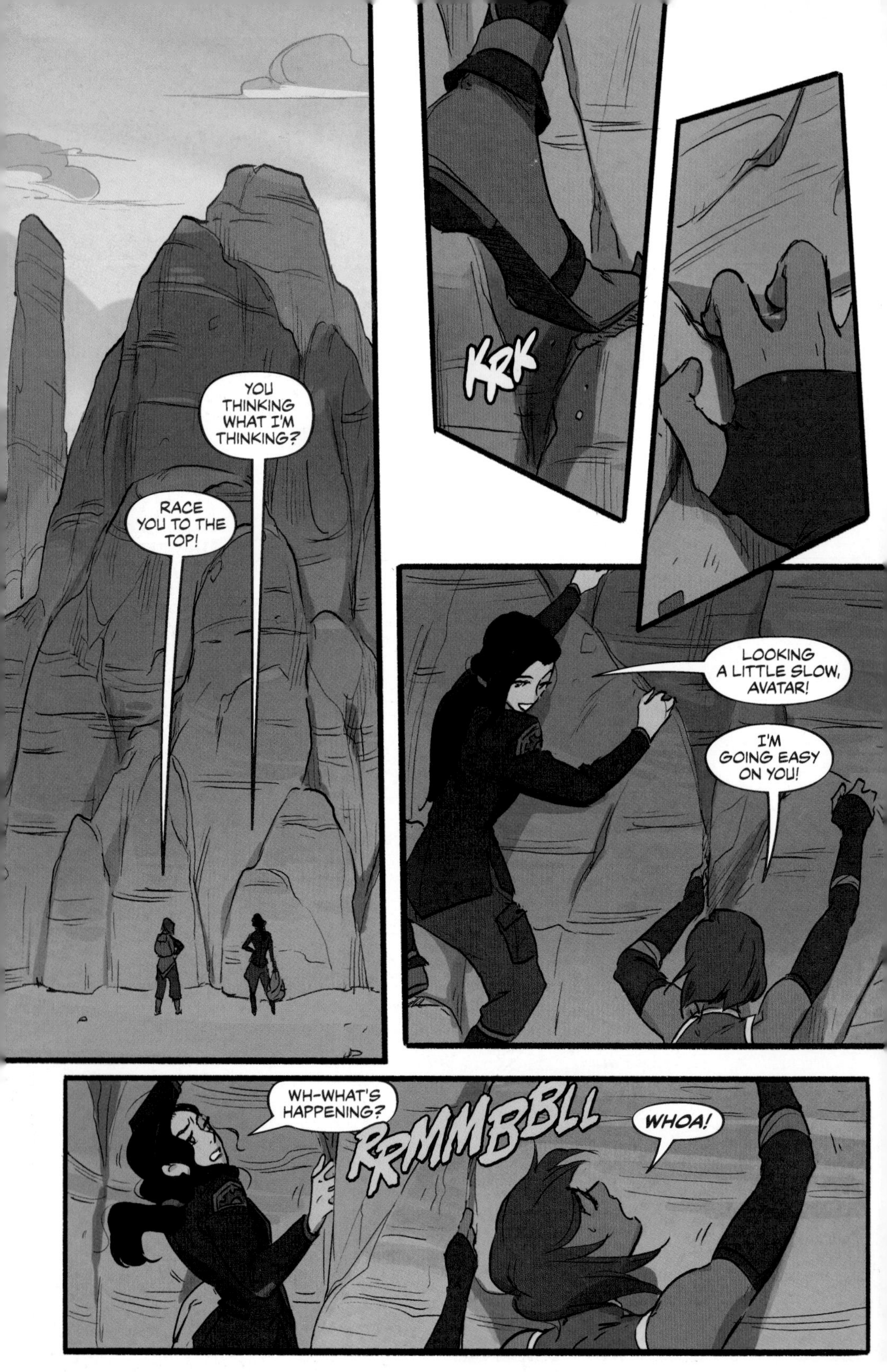
YOU THINKING WHAT I'M THINKING?
RACE YOU TO THE TOP!
KRK
LOOKING A LITTLE SLOW, AVATAR!
I'M GOING EASY ON YOU!
WH-WHAT'S HAPPENING?
RRMMMBBLL
WHOA!

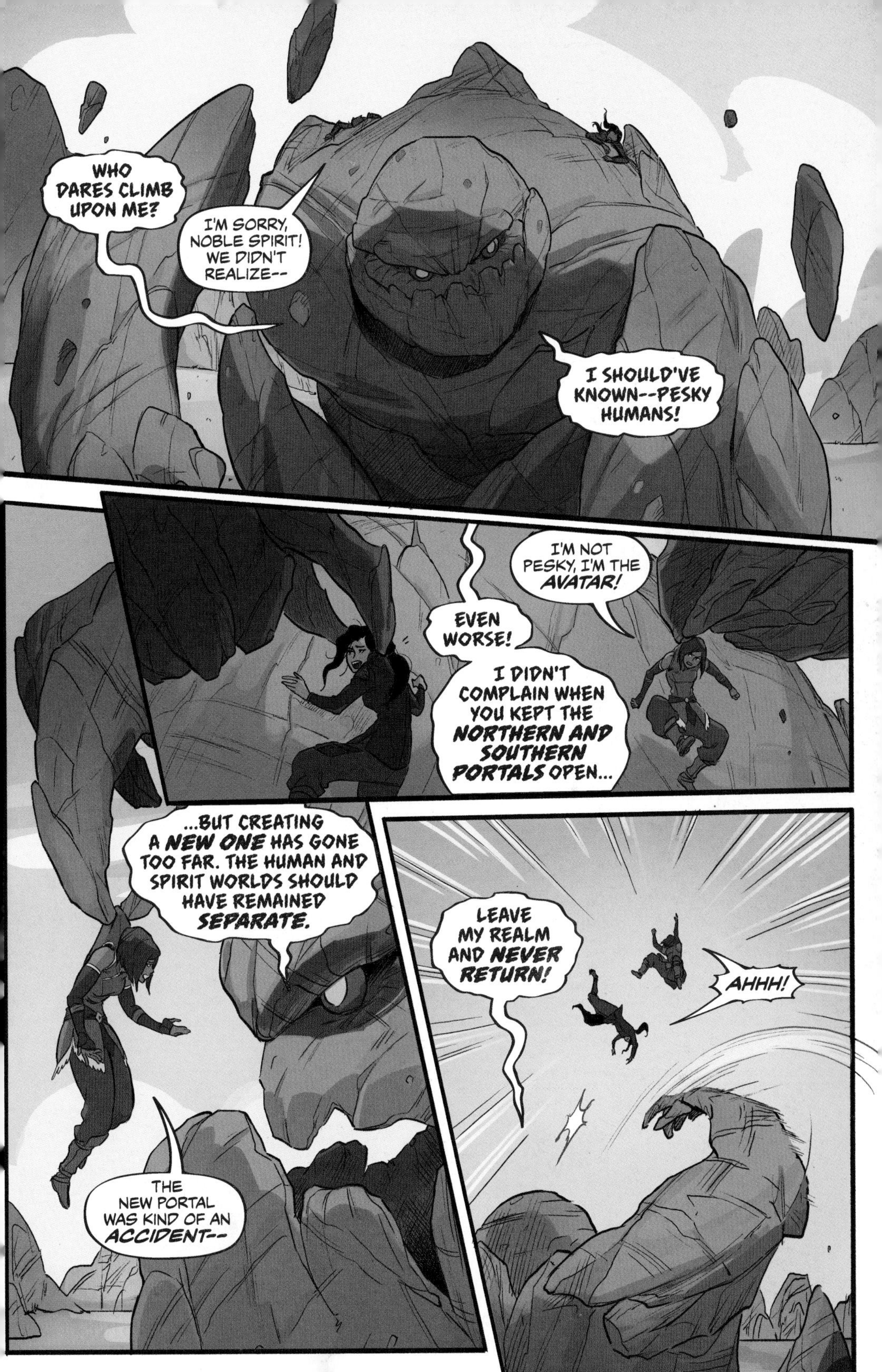
WHO DARES CLIMB UPON ME?
I'M SORRY, NOBLE SPIRIT! WE DIDN'T REALIZE--
I SHOULD'VE KNOWN--PESKY HUMANS!
I'M NOT PESKY, I'M THE AVATAR!
EVEN WORSE!
I DIDN'T COMPLAIN WHEN YOU KEPT THE NORTHERN AND SOUTHERN PORTALS OPEN...
...BUT CREATING A NEW ONE HAS GONE TOO FAR. THE HUMAN AND SPIRIT WORLDS SHOULD HAVE REMAINED SEPARATE.
THE NEW PORTAL WAS KIND OF AN ACCIDENT--
LEAVE MY REALM AND NEVER RETURN!
AHHH!

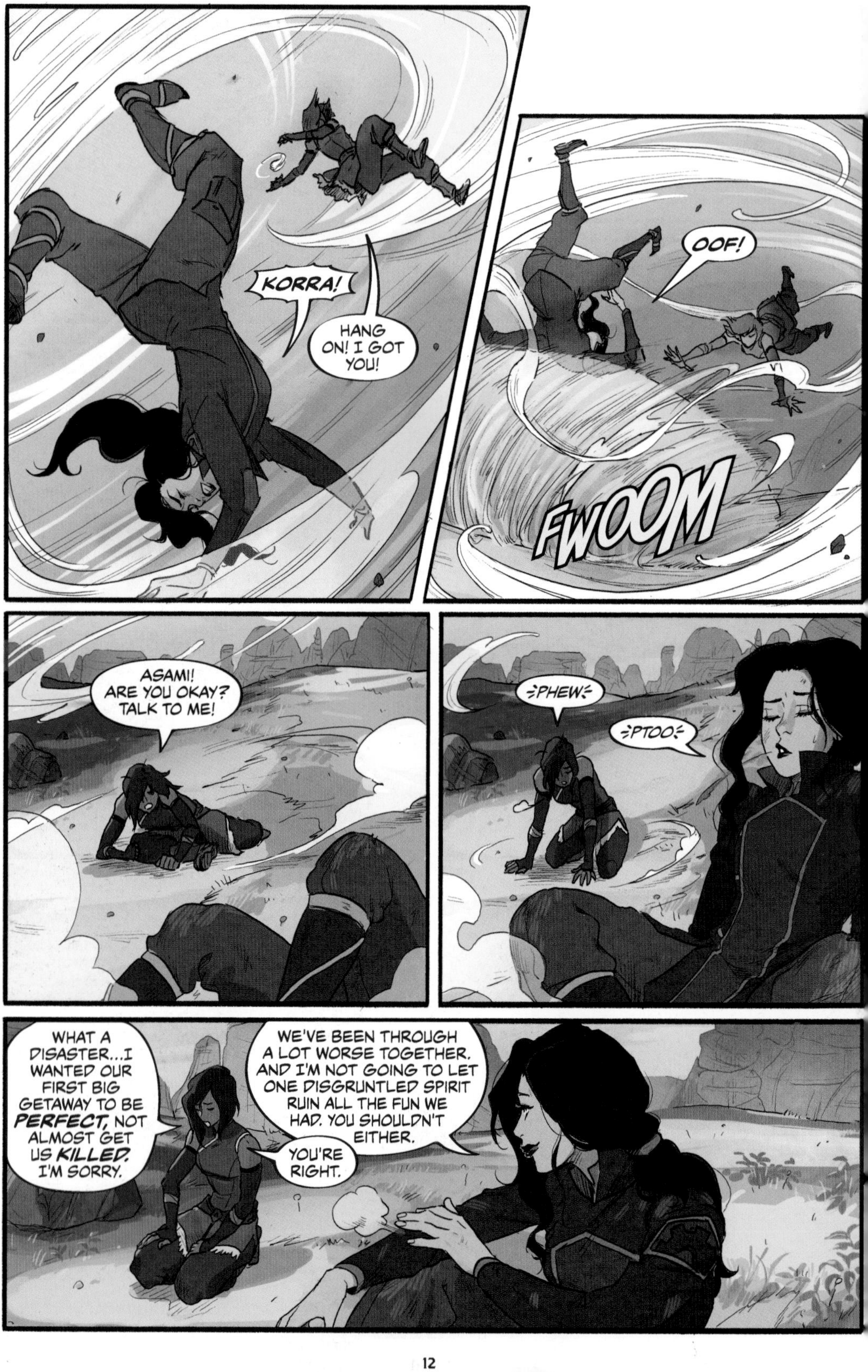

KORRA!
HANG ON! I GOT YOU!
OOF!
FWOOM
ASAMI! ARE YOU OKAY? TALK TO ME!
PHEW
PTOO
WHAT A DISASTER...I WANTED OUR FIRST BIG GETAWAY TO BE PERFECT, NOT ALMOST GET US KILLED. I'M SORRY.
WE'VE BEEN THROUGH A LOT WORSE TOGETHER. AND I'M NOT GOING TO LET ONE DISGRUNTLED SPIRIT RUIN ALL THE FUN WE HAD. YOU SHOULDN'T EITHER.
YOU'RE RIGHT.

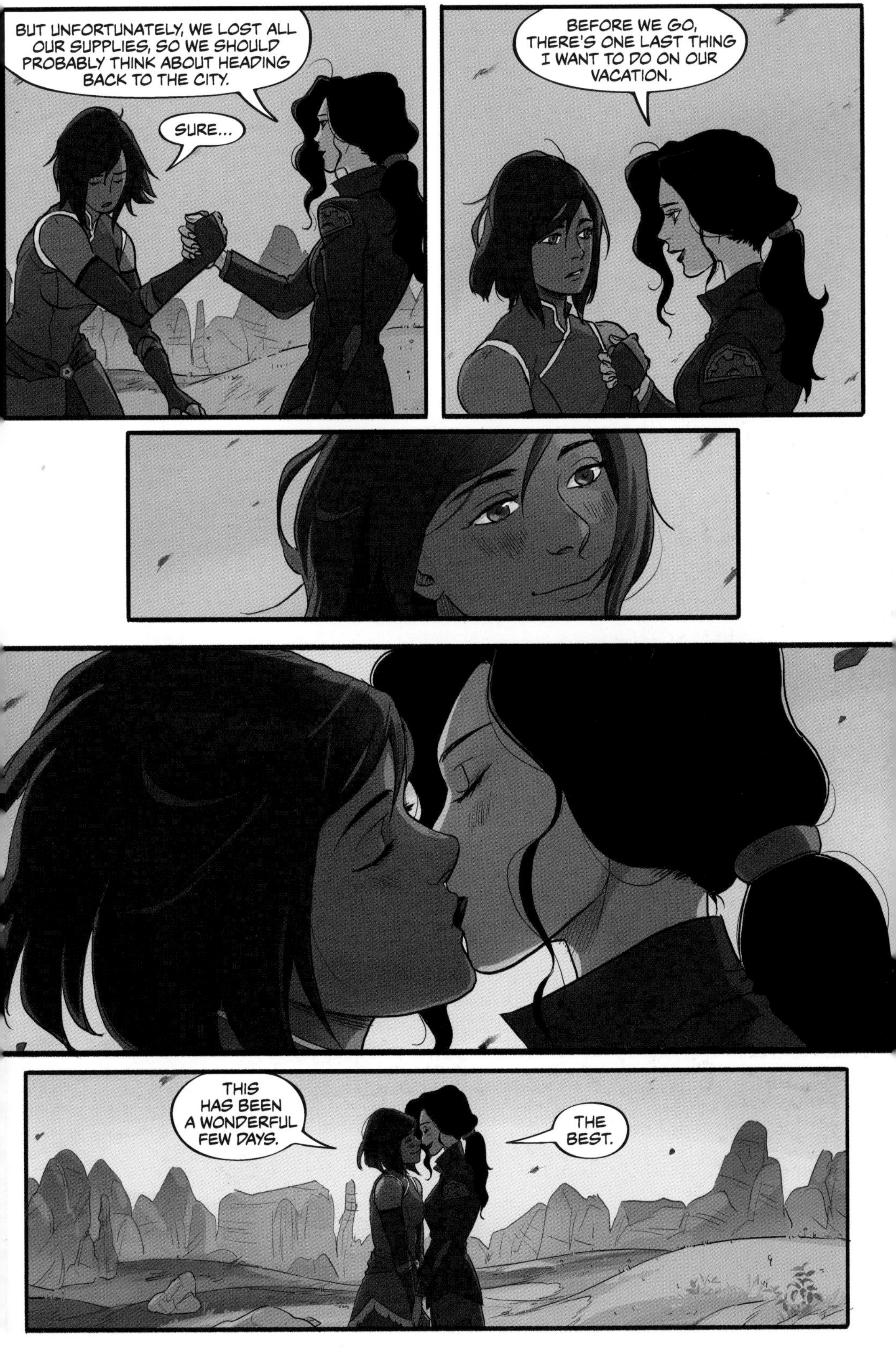
BUT UNFORTUNATELY, WE LOST ALL OUR SUPPLIES, SO WE SHOULD PROBABLY THINK ABOUT HEADING BACK TO THE CITY.
SURE...
BEFORE WE GO, THERE'S ONE LAST THING I WANT TO DO ON OUR VACATION.
THIS HAS BEEN A WONDERFUL FEW DAYS.
THE BEST.

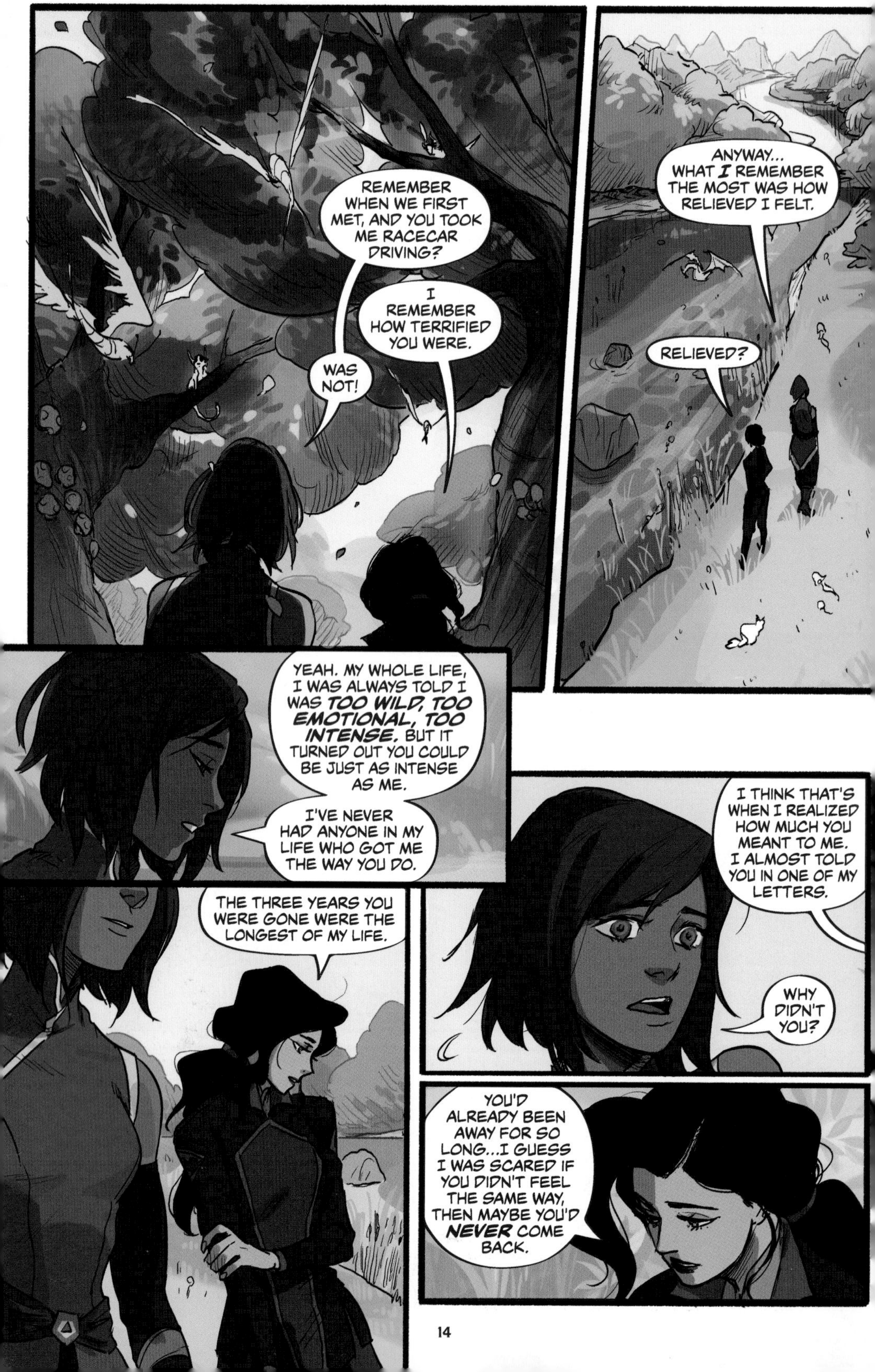
REMEMBER WHEN WE FIRST MET, AND YOU TOOK ME RACECAR DRIVING?
I REMEMBER HOW TERRIFIED YOU WERE.
WAS NOT!
ANYWAY... WHAT I REMEMBER THE MOST WAS HOW RELIEVED I FELT.
RELIEVED?
YEAH. MY WHOLE LIFE, I WAS ALWAYS TOLD I WAS TOO WILD, TOO EMOTIONAL, TOO INTENSE. BUT IT TURNED OUT YOU COULD BE JUST AS INTENSE AS ME.
I'VE NEVER HAD ANYONE IN MY LIFE WHO GOT ME THE WAY YOU DO.
THE THREE YEARS YOU WERE GONE WERE THE LONGEST OF MY LIFE.
I THINK THAT'S WHEN I REALIZED HOW MUCH YOU MEANT TO ME. I ALMOST TOLD YOU IN ONE OF MY LETTERS.
WHY DIDN'T YOU?
YOU'D ALREADY BEEN AWAY FOR SO LONG...I GUESS I WAS SCARED IF YOU DIDN'T FEEL THE SAME WAY, THEN MAYBE YOU'D NEVER COME BACK.

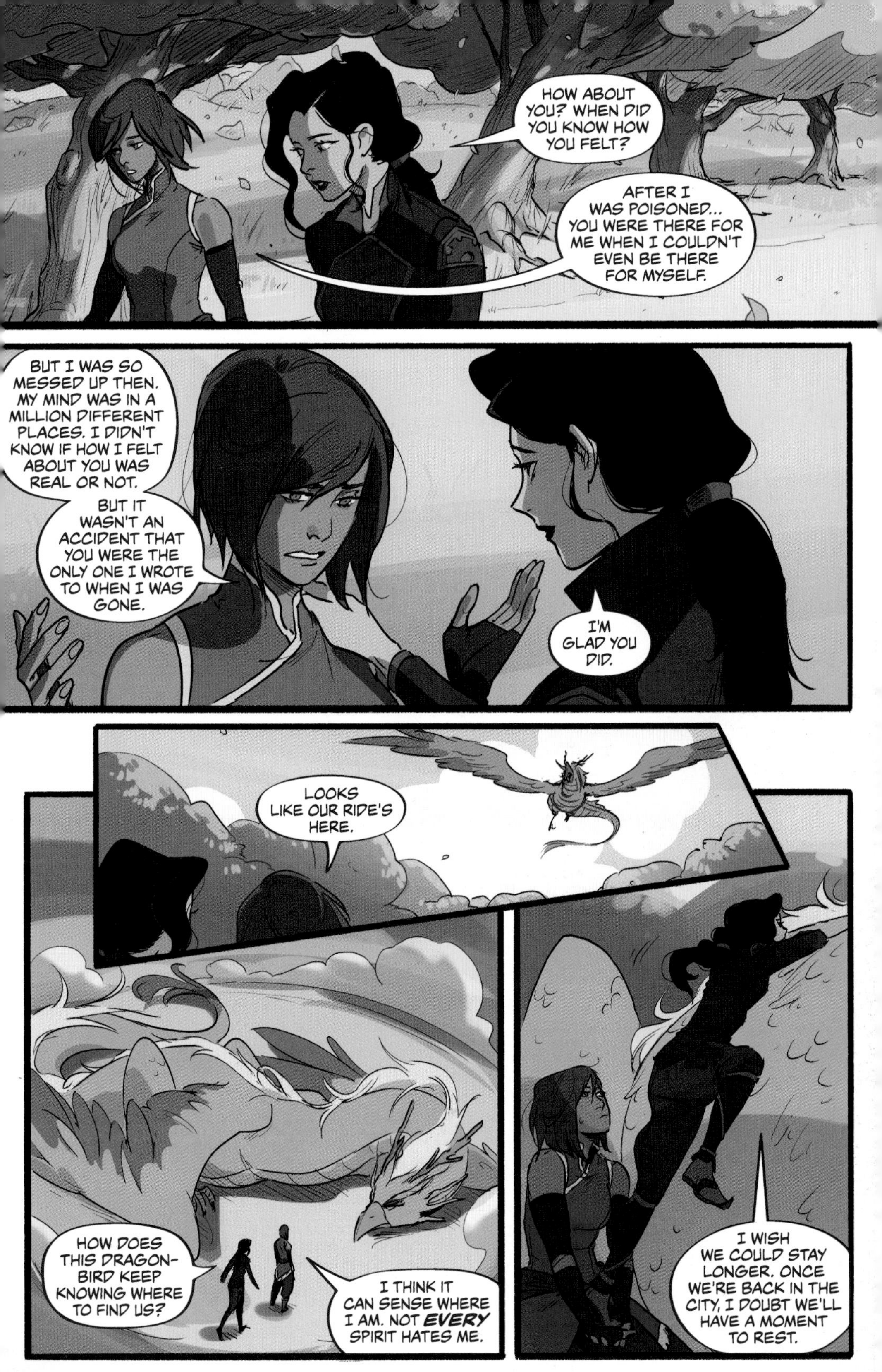
HOW ABOUT YOU? WHEN DID YOU KNOW HOW YOU FELT?
AFTER I WAS POISONED... YOU WERE THERE FOR ME WHEN I COULDN'T EVEN BE THERE FOR MYSELF.
BUT I WAS SO MESSED UP THEN. MY MIND WAS IN A MILLION DIFFERENT PLACES. I DIDN'T KNOW IF HOW I FELT ABOUT YOU WAS REAL OR NOT.
BUT IT WASN'T AN ACCIDENT THAT YOU WERE THE ONLY ONE I WROTE TO WHEN I WAS GONE.
I'M GLAD YOU DID.
LOOKS LIKE OUR RIDE'S HERE.
HOW DOES THIS DRAGON-BIRD KEEP KNOWING WHERE TO FIND US?
I THINK IT CAN SENSE WHERE I AM. NOT EVERY SPIRIT HATES ME.
I WISH WE COULD STAY LONGER. ONCE WE'RE BACK IN THE CITY, I DOUBT WE'LL HAVE A MOMENT TO REST.

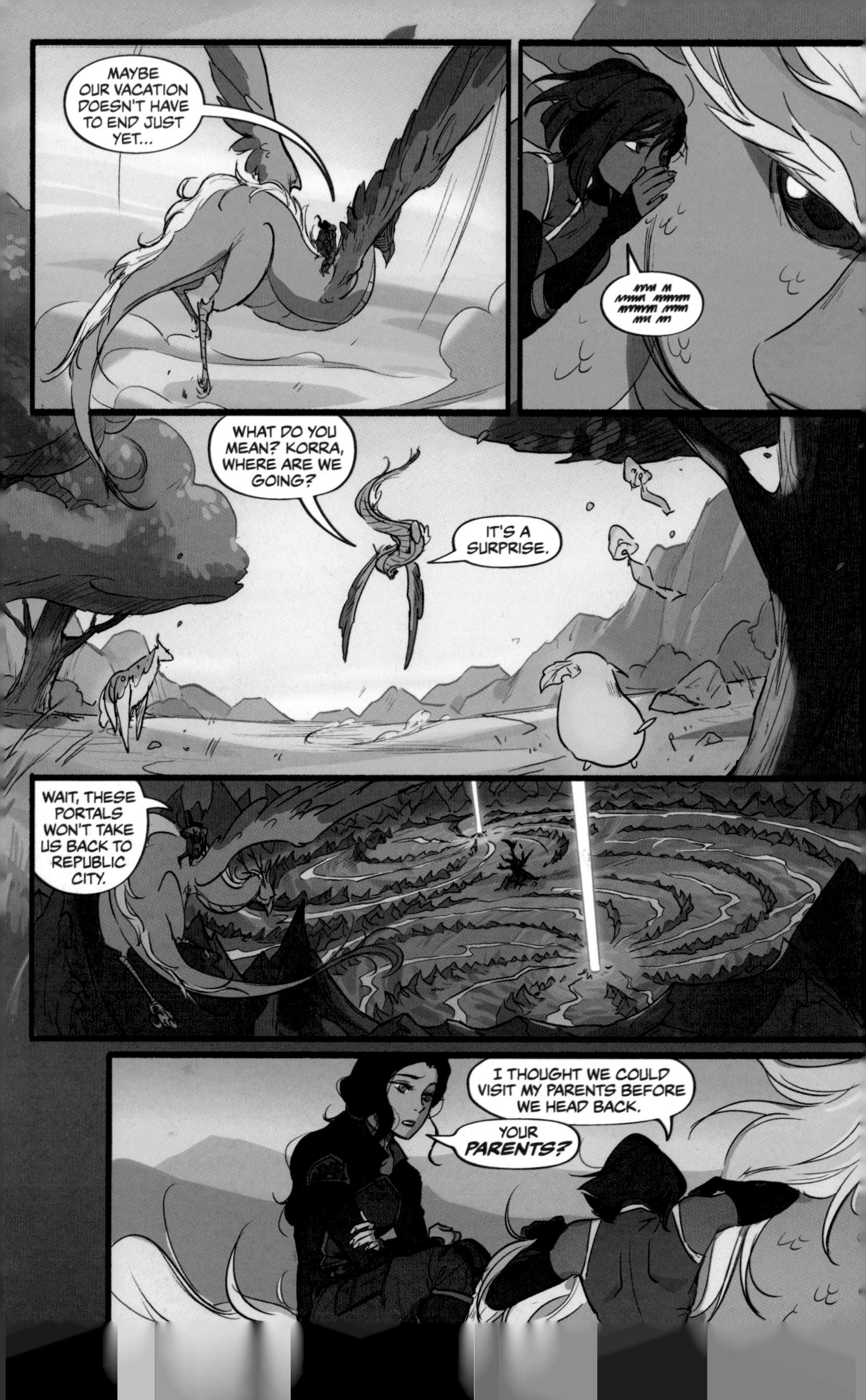
MAYBE OUR VACATION DOESN'T HAVE TO END JUST YET...
WHAT DO YOU MEAN? KORRA, WHERE ARE WE GOING?
IT'S A SURPRISE.
WAIT, THESE PORTALS WON'T TAKE US BACK TO REPUBLIC CITY.
I THOUGHT WE COULD VISIT MY PARENTS BEFORE WE HEAD BACK.
YOUR *PARENTS?*

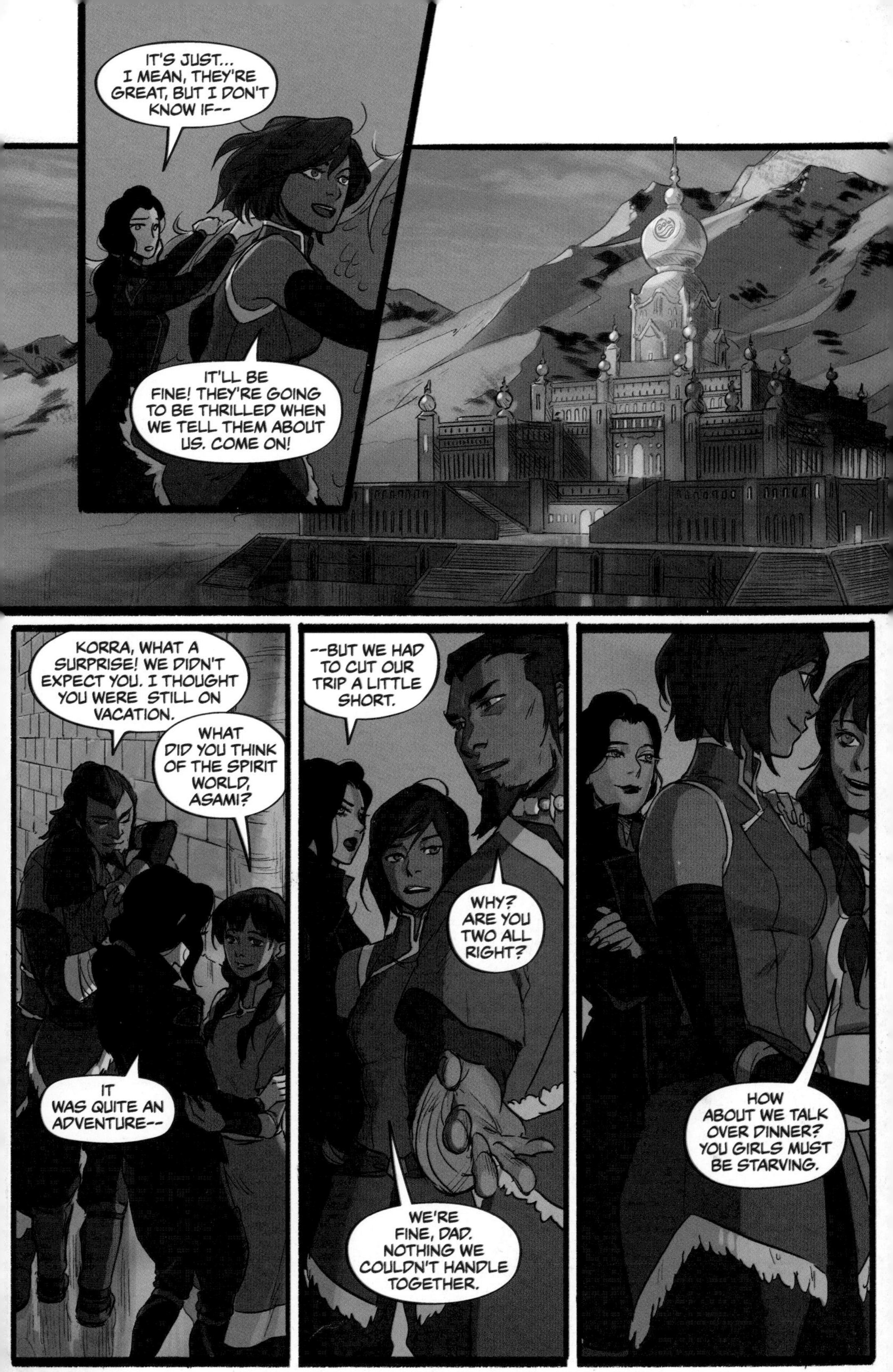
IT'S JUST... I MEAN, THEY'RE GREAT, BUT I DON'T KNOW IF--
IT'LL BE FINE! THEY'RE GOING TO BE THRILLED WHEN WE TELL THEM ABOUT US. COME ON!
KORRA, WHAT A SURPRISE! WE DIDN'T EXPECT YOU. I THOUGHT YOU WERE STILL ON VACATION.
WHAT DID YOU THINK OF THE SPIRIT WORLD, ASAMI?
IT WAS QUITE AN ADVENTURE--
--BUT WE HAD TO CUT OUR TRIP A LITTLE SHORT.
WHY? ARE YOU TWO ALL RIGHT?
WE'RE FINE, DAD. NOTHING WE COULDN'T HANDLE TOGETHER.
HOW ABOUT WE TALK OVER DINNER? YOU GIRLS MUST BE STARVING.

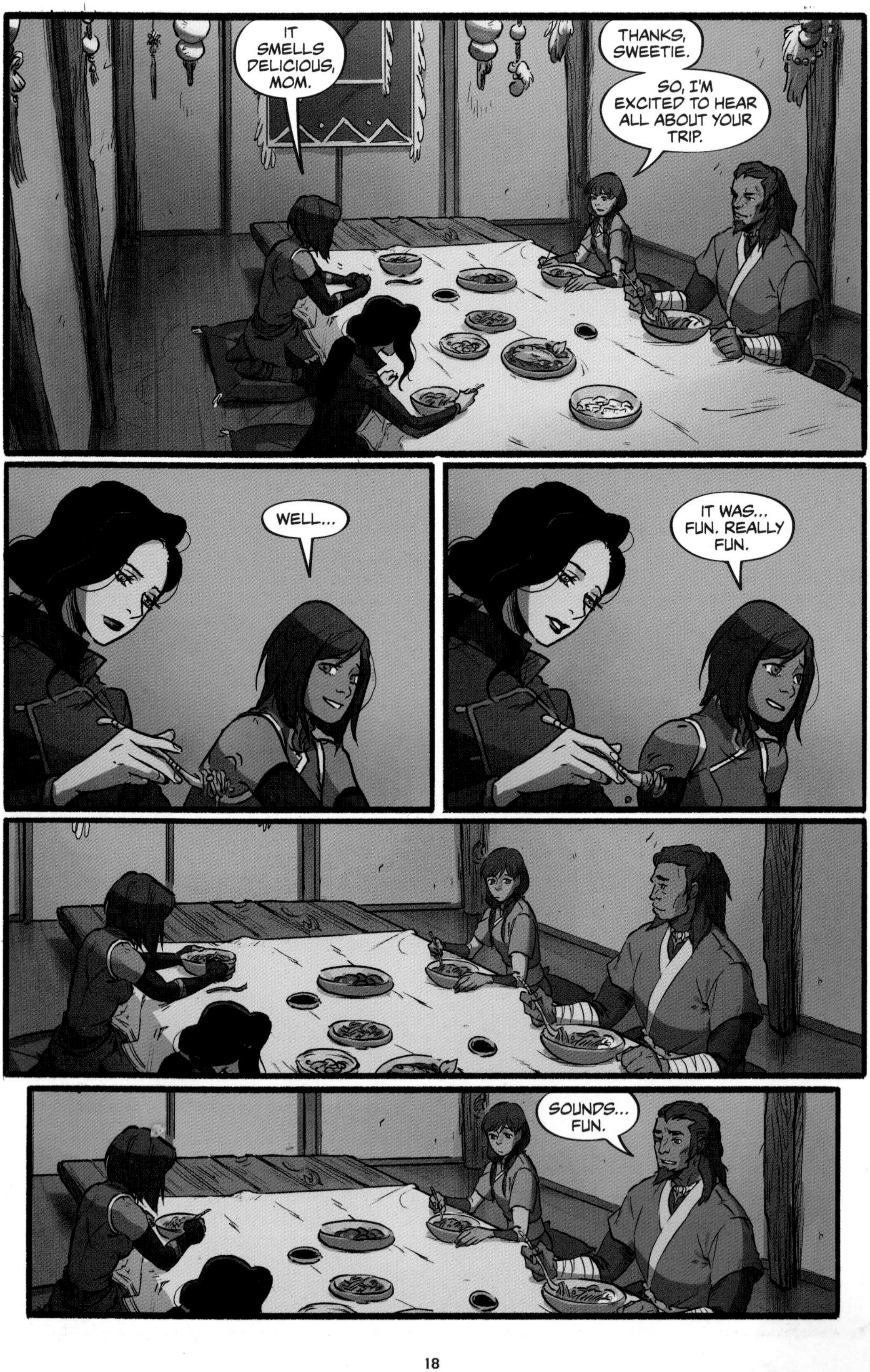
IT SMELLS DELICIOUS, MOM.
THANKS, SWEETIE.
SO, I'M EXCITED TO HEAR ALL ABOUT YOUR TRIP.
WELL...
IT WAS... FUN. REALLY FUN.
SOUNDS... FUN.

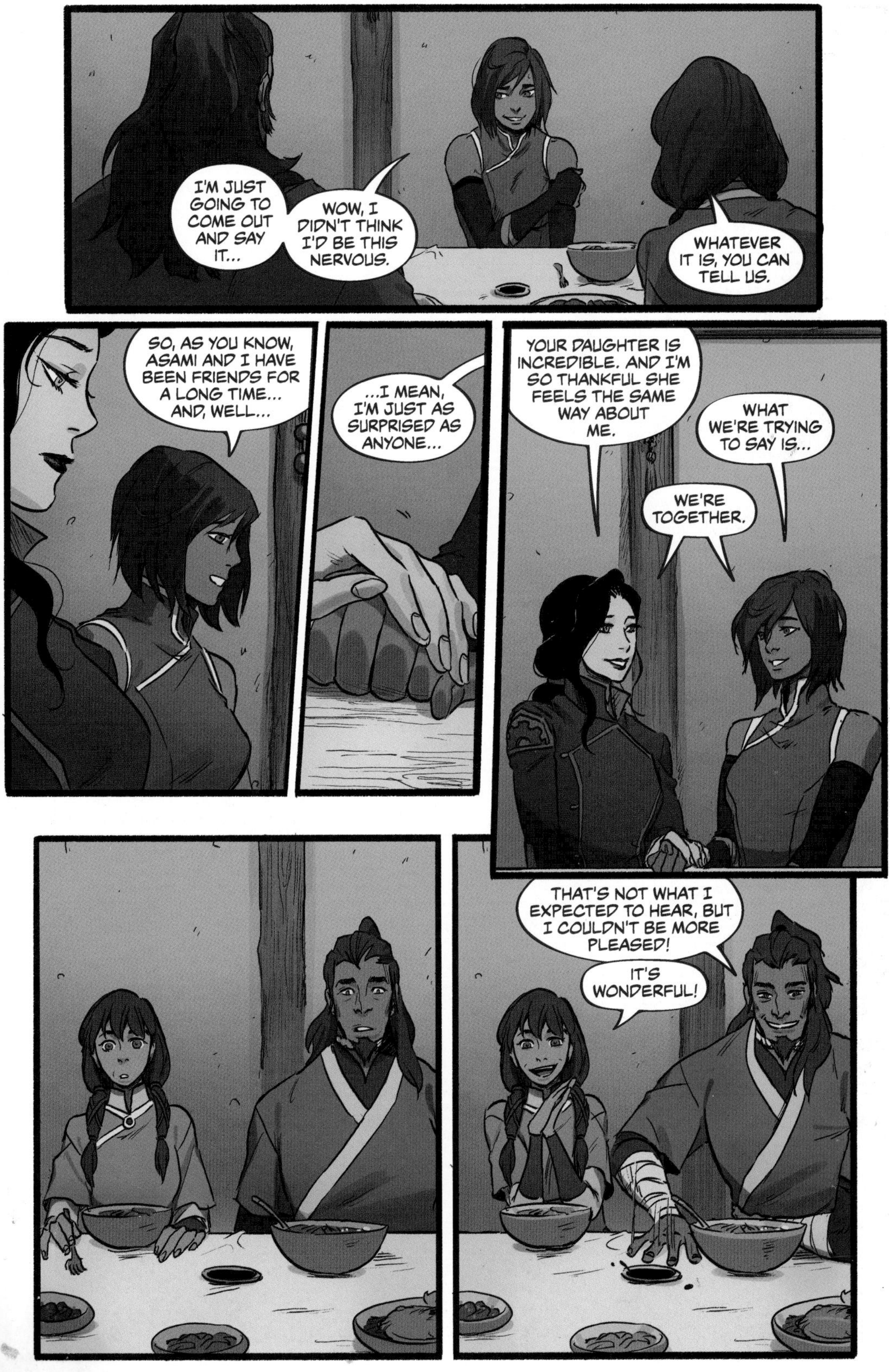
I'M JUST GOING TO COME OUT AND SAY IT...
WOW, I DIDN'T THINK I'D BE THIS NERVOUS.
WHATEVER IT IS, YOU CAN TELL US.
SO, AS YOU KNOW, ASAMI AND I HAVE BEEN FRIENDS FOR A LONG TIME... AND, WELL...
...I MEAN, I'M JUST AS SURPRISED AS ANYONE...
YOUR DAUGHTER IS INCREDIBLE. AND I'M SO THANKFUL SHE FEELS THE SAME WAY ABOUT ME.
WHAT WE'RE TRYING TO SAY IS...
WE'RE TOGETHER.
THAT'S NOT WHAT I EXPECTED TO HEAR, BUT I COULDN'T BE MORE PLEASED!
IT'S WONDERFUL!

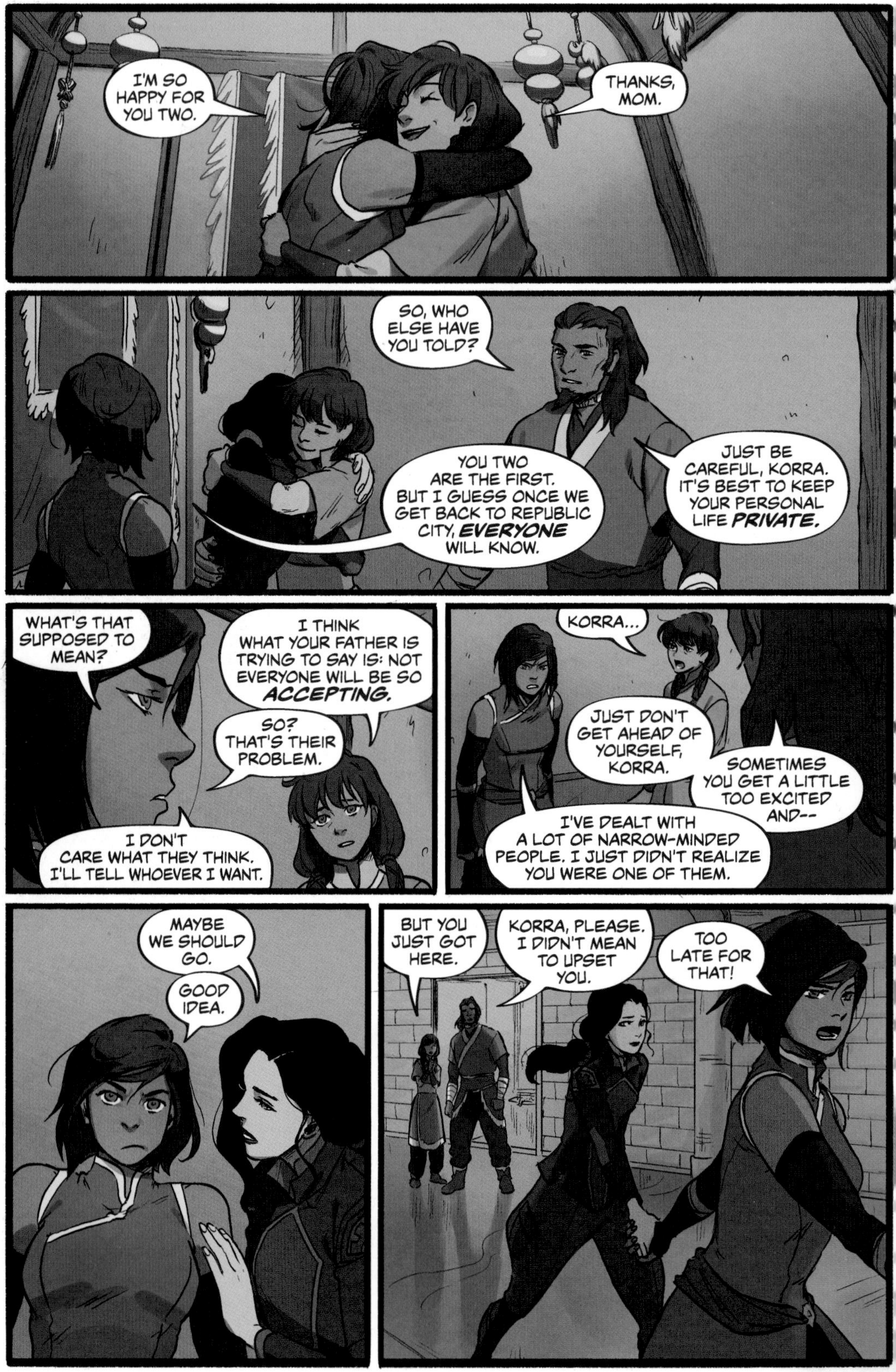
I'M SO HAPPY FOR YOU TWO.
THANKS, MOM.
SO, WHO ELSE HAVE YOU TOLD?
YOU TWO ARE THE FIRST. BUT I GUESS ONCE WE GET BACK TO REPUBLIC CITY, EVERYONE WILL KNOW.
JUST BE CAREFUL, KORRA. IT'S BEST TO KEEP YOUR PERSONAL LIFE PRIVATE.
WHAT'S THAT SUPPOSED TO MEAN?
I THINK WHAT YOUR FATHER IS TRYING TO SAY IS: NOT EVERYONE WILL BE SO ACCEPTING.
SO? THAT'S THEIR PROBLEM.
I DON'T CARE WHAT THEY THINK. I'LL TELL WHOEVER I WANT.
KORRA...
JUST DON'T GET AHEAD OF YOURSELF, KORRA.
SOMETIMES YOU GET A LITTLE TOO EXCITED AND--
I'VE DEALT WITH A LOT OF NARROW-MINDED PEOPLE. I JUST DIDN'T REALIZE YOU WERE ONE OF THEM.
MAYBE WE SHOULD GO.
GOOD IDEA.
BUT YOU JUST GOT HERE.
KORRA, PLEASE. I DIDN'T MEAN TO UPSET YOU.
TOO LATE FOR THAT!

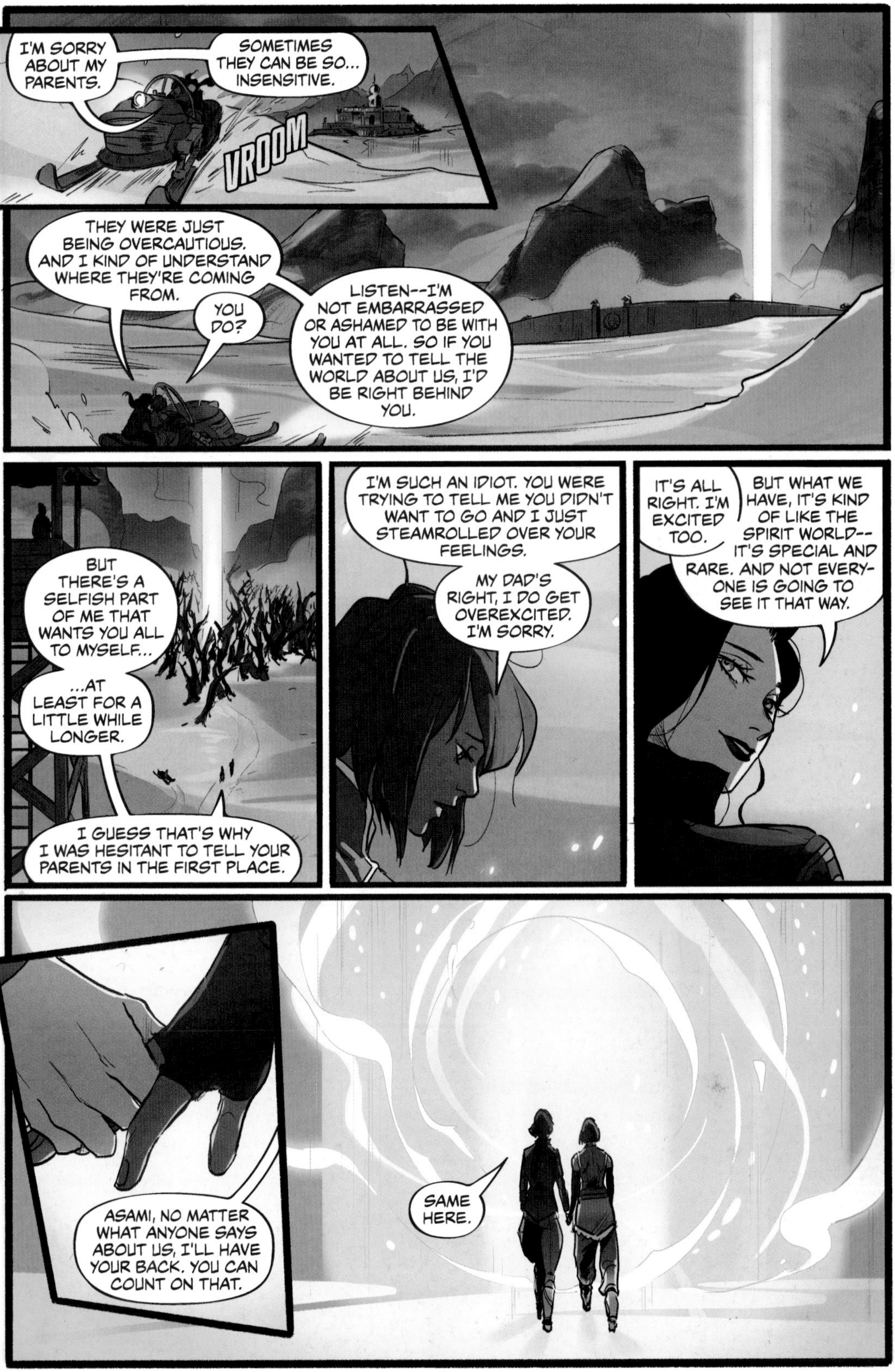

I'M SORRY ABOUT MY PARENTS.
SOMETIMES THEY CAN BE SO... INSENSITIVE.
VROOM
THEY WERE JUST BEING OVERCAUTIOUS. AND I KIND OF UNDERSTAND WHERE THEY'RE COMING FROM.
YOU DO?
LISTEN--I'M NOT EMBARRASSED OR ASHAMED TO BE WITH YOU AT ALL. SO IF YOU WANTED TO TELL THE WORLD ABOUT US, I'D BE RIGHT BEHIND YOU.
BUT THERE'S A SELFISH PART OF ME THAT WANTS YOU ALL TO MYSELF...
...AT LEAST FOR A LITTLE WHILE LONGER.
I GUESS THAT'S WHY I WAS HESITANT TO TELL YOUR PARENTS IN THE FIRST PLACE.
I'M SUCH AN IDIOT. YOU WERE TRYING TO TELL ME YOU DIDN'T WANT TO GO AND I JUST STEAMROLLED OVER YOUR FEELINGS.
MY DAD'S RIGHT, I DO GET OVEREXCITED. I'M SORRY.
IT'S ALL RIGHT. I'M EXCITED TOO.
BUT WHAT WE HAVE, IT'S KIND OF LIKE THE SPIRIT WORLD-- IT'S SPECIAL AND RARE. AND NOT EVERY-ONE IS GOING TO SEE IT THAT WAY.
ASAMI, NO MATTER WHAT ANYONE SAYS ABOUT US, I'LL HAVE YOUR BACK. YOU CAN COUNT ON THAT.
SAME HERE.

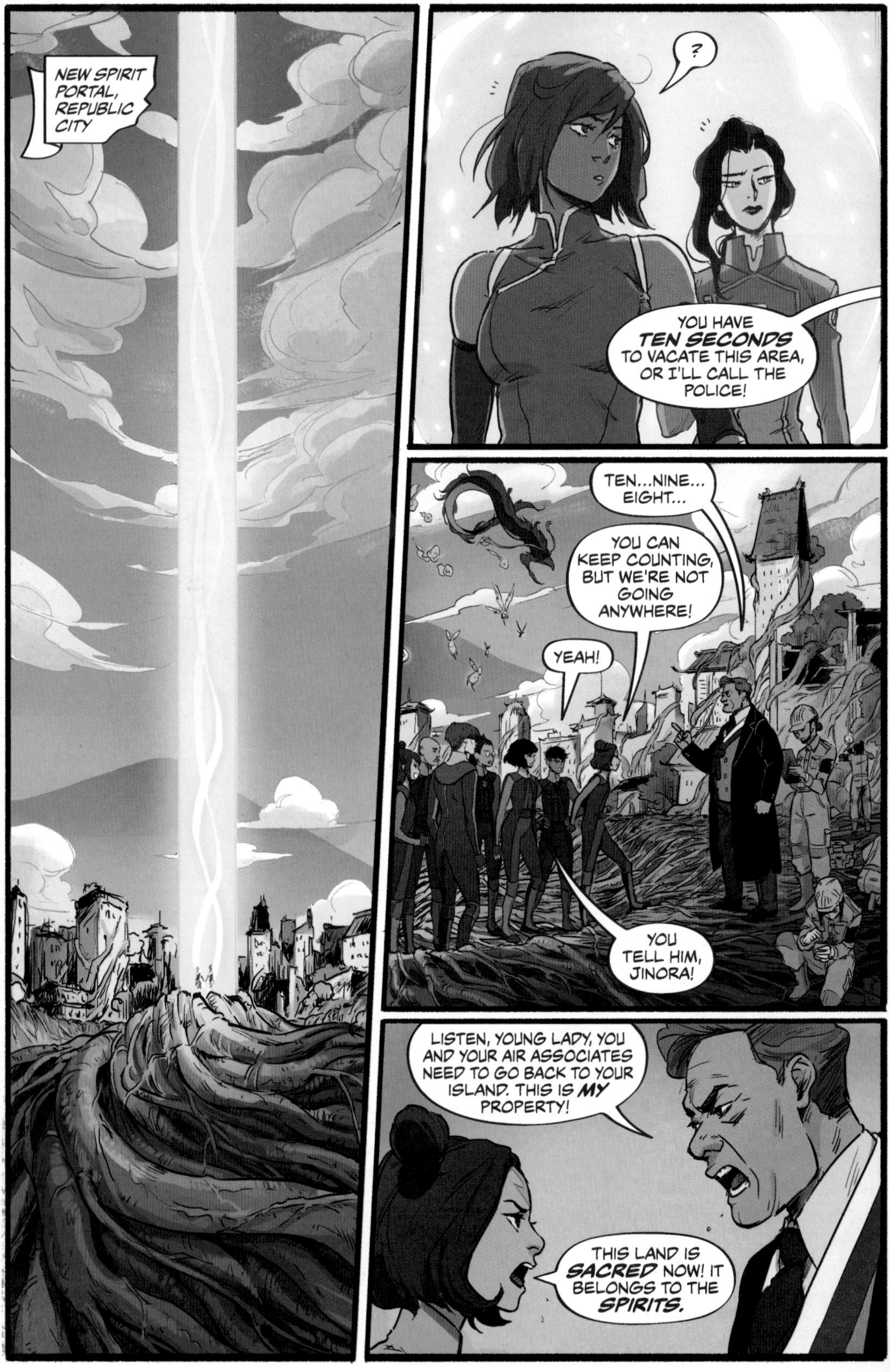

NEW SPIRIT PORTAL, REPUBLIC CITY
?
YOU HAVE TEN SECONDS TO VACATE THIS AREA, OR I'LL CALL THE POLICE!
TEN...NINE... EIGHT...
YOU CAN KEEP COUNTING, BUT WE'RE NOT GOING ANYWHERE!
YEAH!
YOU TELL HIM, JINORA!
LISTEN, YOUNG LADY, YOU AND YOUR AIR ASSOCIATES NEED TO GO BACK TO YOUR ISLAND. THIS IS MY PROPERTY!
THIS LAND IS SACRED NOW! IT BELONGS TO THE SPIRITS.

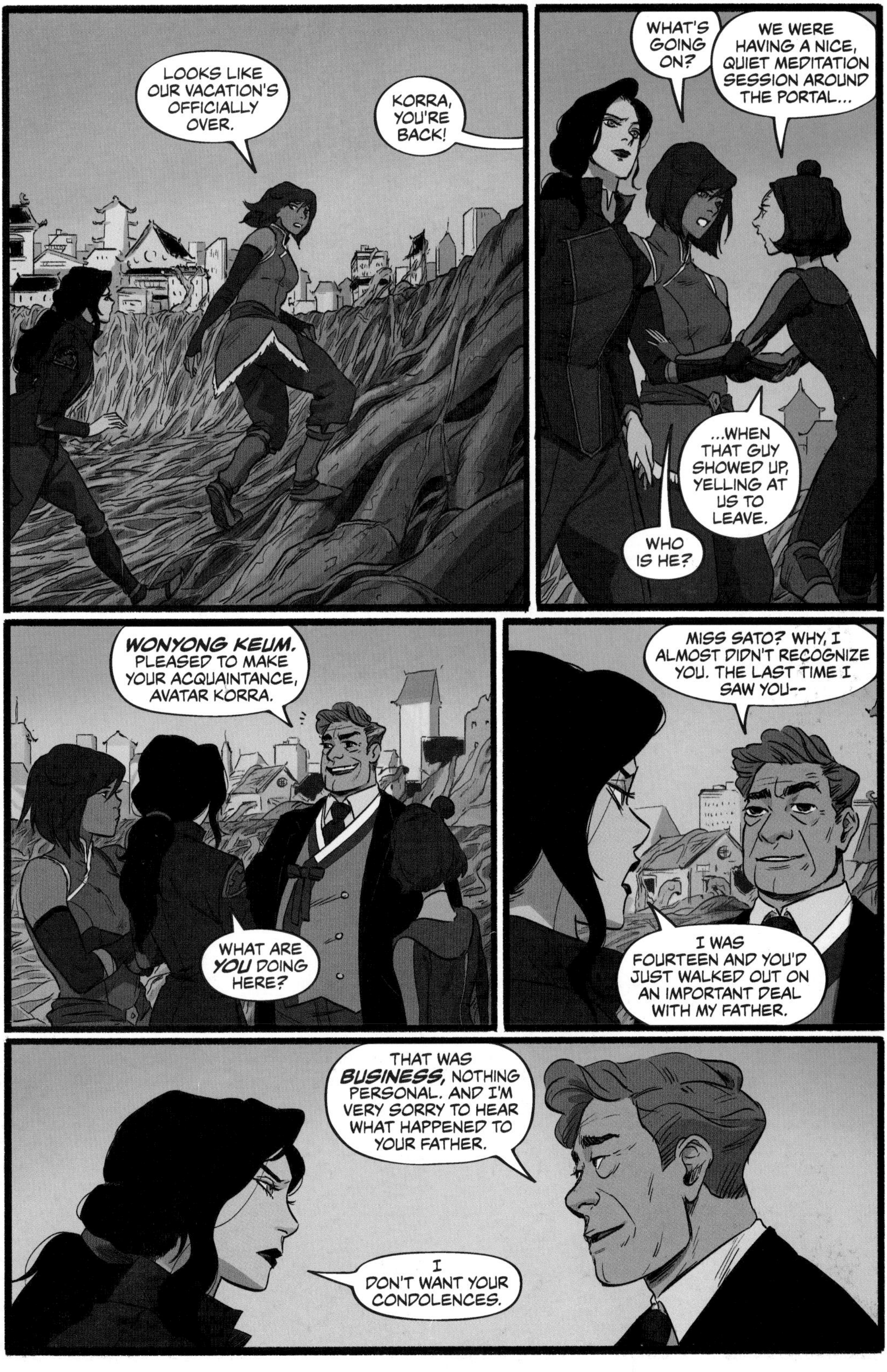
LOOKS LIKE OUR VACATION'S OFFICIALLY OVER.
KORRA, YOU'RE BACK!
WHAT'S GOING ON?
WE WERE HAVING A NICE, QUIET MEDITATION SESSION AROUND THE PORTAL...
...WHEN THAT GUY SHOWED UP, YELLING AT US TO LEAVE.
WHO IS HE?
WONYONG KEUM. PLEASED TO MAKE YOUR ACQUAINTANCE, AVATAR KORRA.
WHAT ARE YOU DOING HERE?
MISS SATO? WHY, I ALMOST DIDN'T RECOGNIZE YOU. THE LAST TIME I SAW YOU--
I WAS FOURTEEN AND YOU'D JUST WALKED OUT ON AN IMPORTANT DEAL WITH MY FATHER.
THAT WAS BUSINESS, NOTHING PERSONAL. AND I'M VERY SORRY TO HEAR WHAT HAPPENED TO YOUR FATHER.
I DON'T WANT YOUR CONDOLENCES.

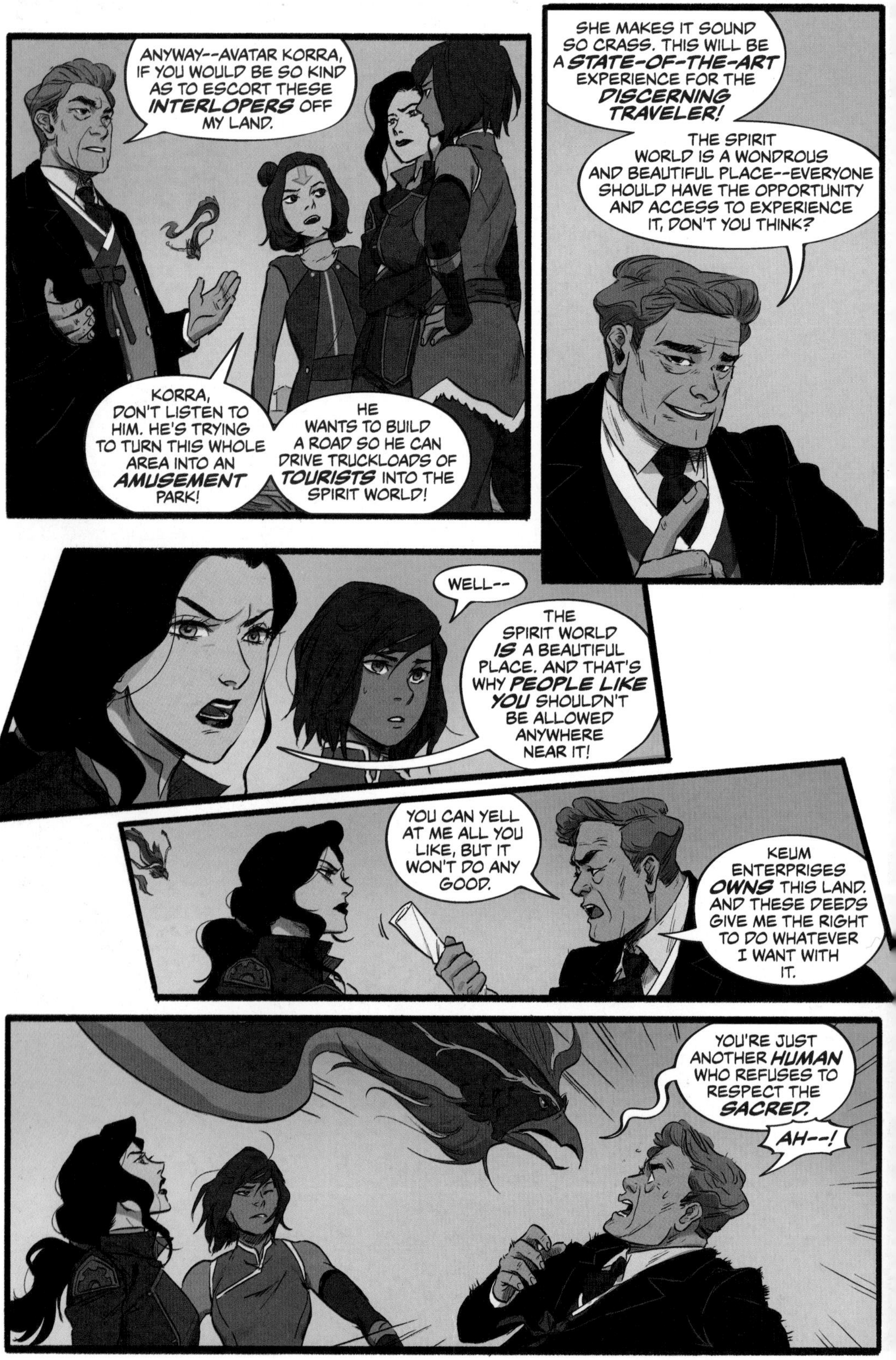
ANYWAY--AVATAR KORRA, IF YOU WOULD BE SO KIND AS TO ESCORT THESE INTERLOPERS OFF MY LAND.
KORRA, DON'T LISTEN TO HIM. HE'S TRYING TO TURN THIS WHOLE AREA INTO AN AMUSEMENT PARK!
HE WANTS TO BUILD A ROAD SO HE CAN DRIVE TRUCKLOADS OF TOURISTS INTO THE SPIRIT WORLD!
SHE MAKES IT SOUND SO CRASS. THIS WILL BE A STATE-OF-THE-ART EXPERIENCE FOR THE DISCERNING TRAVELER!
THE SPIRIT WORLD IS A WONDROUS AND BEAUTIFUL PLACE--EVERYONE SHOULD HAVE THE OPPORTUNITY AND ACCESS TO EXPERIENCE IT, DON'T YOU THINK?
WELL--
THE SPIRIT WORLD IS A BEAUTIFUL PLACE. AND THAT'S WHY PEOPLE LIKE YOU SHOULDN'T BE ALLOWED ANYWHERE NEAR IT!
YOU CAN YELL AT ME ALL YOU LIKE, BUT IT WON'T DO ANY GOOD.
KEUM ENTERPRISES OWNS THIS LAND. AND THESE DEEDS GIVE ME THE RIGHT TO DO WHATEVER I WANT WITH IT.
YOU'RE JUST ANOTHER HUMAN WHO REFUSES TO RESPECT THE SACRED.
AH--!

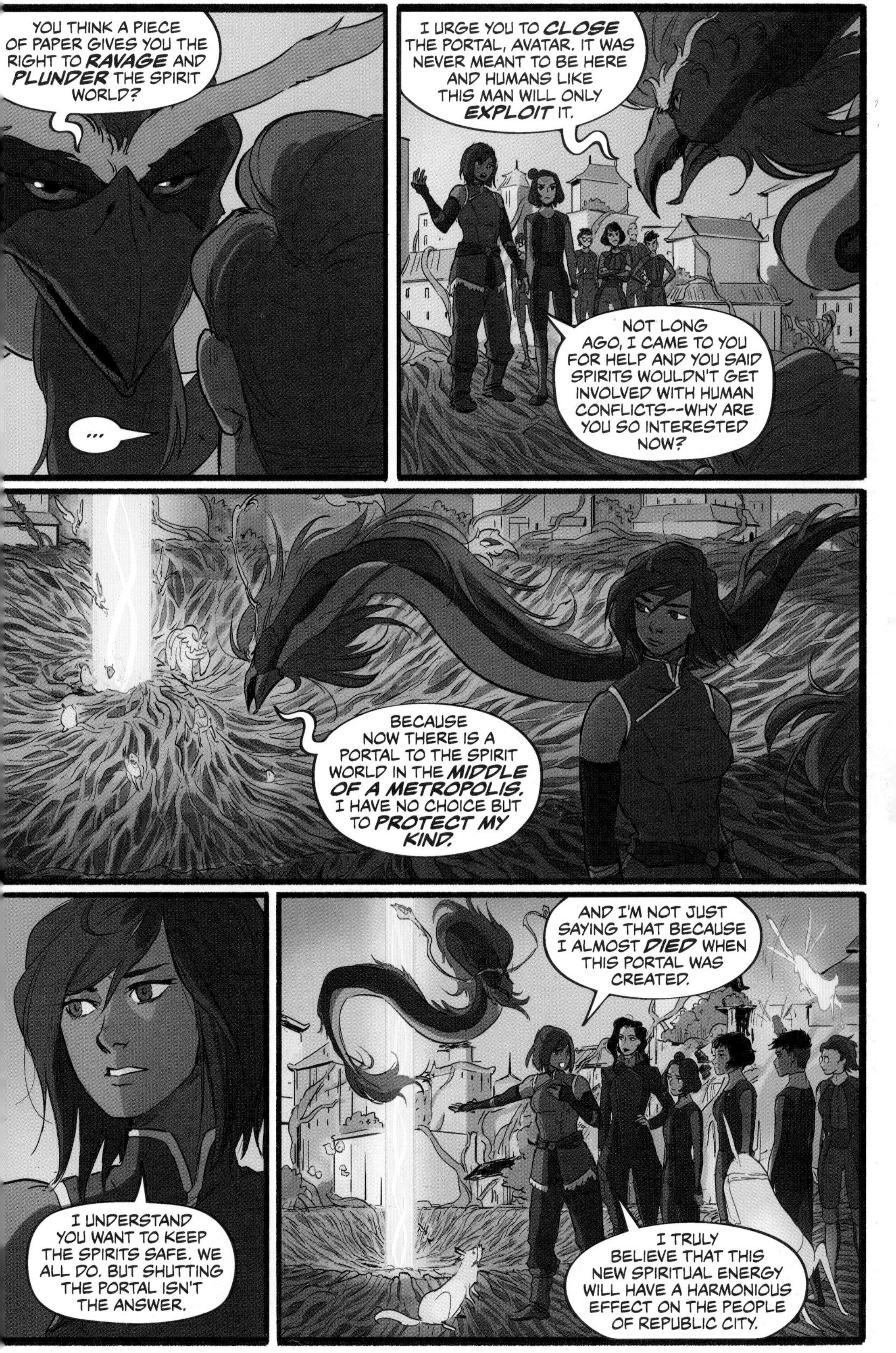
YOU THINK A PIECE OF PAPER GIVES YOU THE RIGHT TO RAVAGE AND PLUNDER THE SPIRIT WORLD?
...
I URGE YOU TO CLOSE THE PORTAL, AVATAR. IT WAS NEVER MEANT TO BE HERE AND HUMANS LIKE THIS MAN WILL ONLY EXPLOIT IT.
NOT LONG AGO, I CAME TO YOU FOR HELP AND YOU SAID SPIRITS WOULDN'T GET INVOLVED WITH HUMAN CONFLICTS--WHY ARE YOU SO INTERESTED NOW?
BECAUSE NOW THERE IS A PORTAL TO THE SPIRIT WORLD IN THE MIDDLE OF A METROPOLIS. I HAVE NO CHOICE BUT TO PROTECT MY KIND.
I UNDERSTAND YOU WANT TO KEEP THE SPIRITS SAFE. WE ALL DO. BUT SHUTTING THE PORTAL ISN'T THE ANSWER.
AND I'M NOT JUST SAYING THAT BECAUSE I ALMOST DIED WHEN THIS PORTAL WAS CREATED.
I TRULY BELIEVE THAT THIS NEW SPIRITUAL ENERGY WILL HAVE A HARMONIOUS EFFECT ON THE PEOPLE OF REPUBLIC CITY.

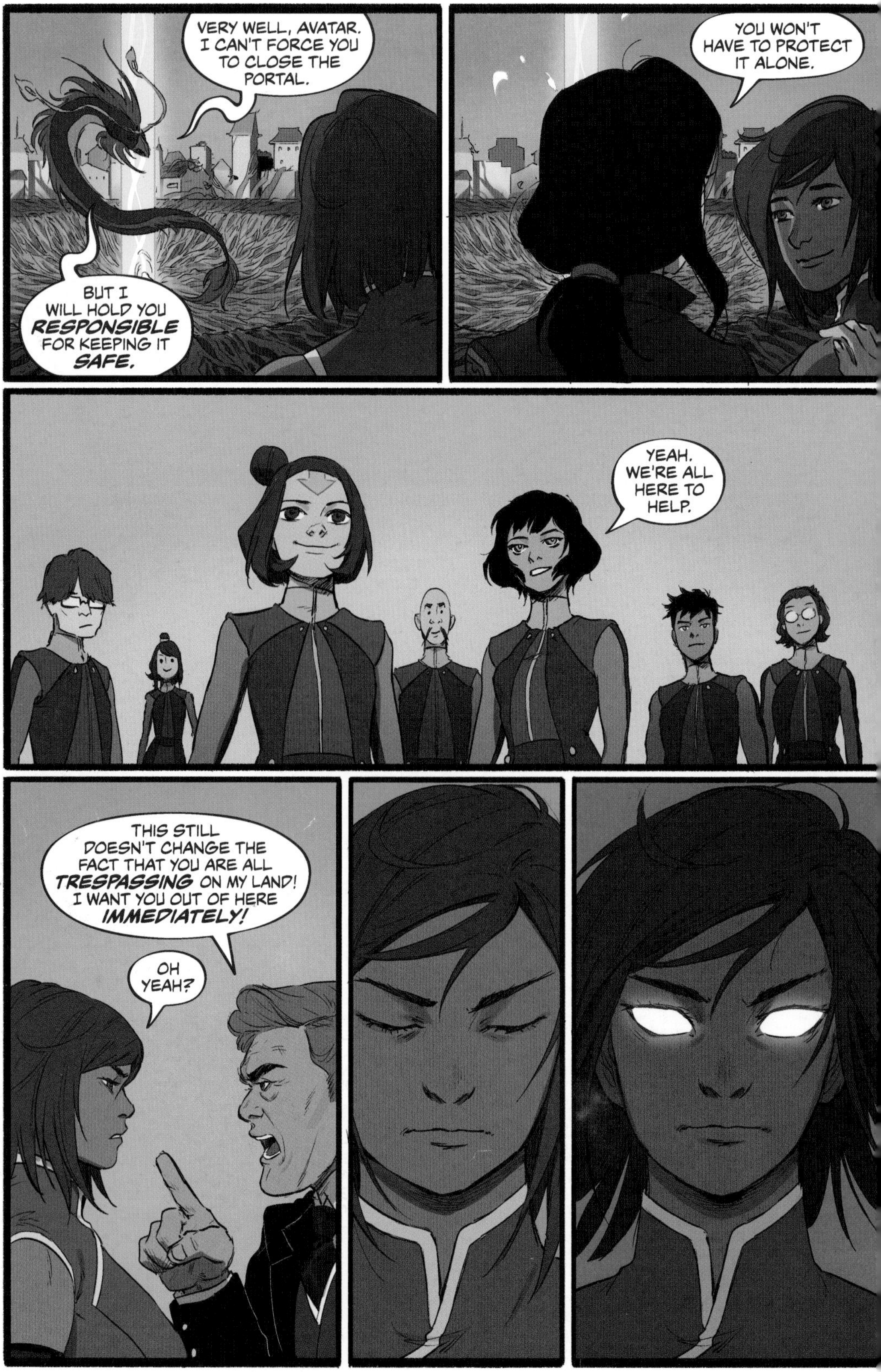
VERY WELL, AVATAR. I CAN'T FORCE YOU TO CLOSE THE PORTAL.
BUT I WILL HOLD YOU RESPONSIBLE FOR KEEPING IT SAFE.
YOU WON'T HAVE TO PROTECT IT ALONE.
YEAH. WE'RE ALL HERE TO HELP.
THIS STILL DOESN'T CHANGE THE FACT THAT YOU ARE ALL TRESPASSING ON MY LAND! I WANT YOU OUT OF HERE IMMEDIATELY!
OH YEAH?

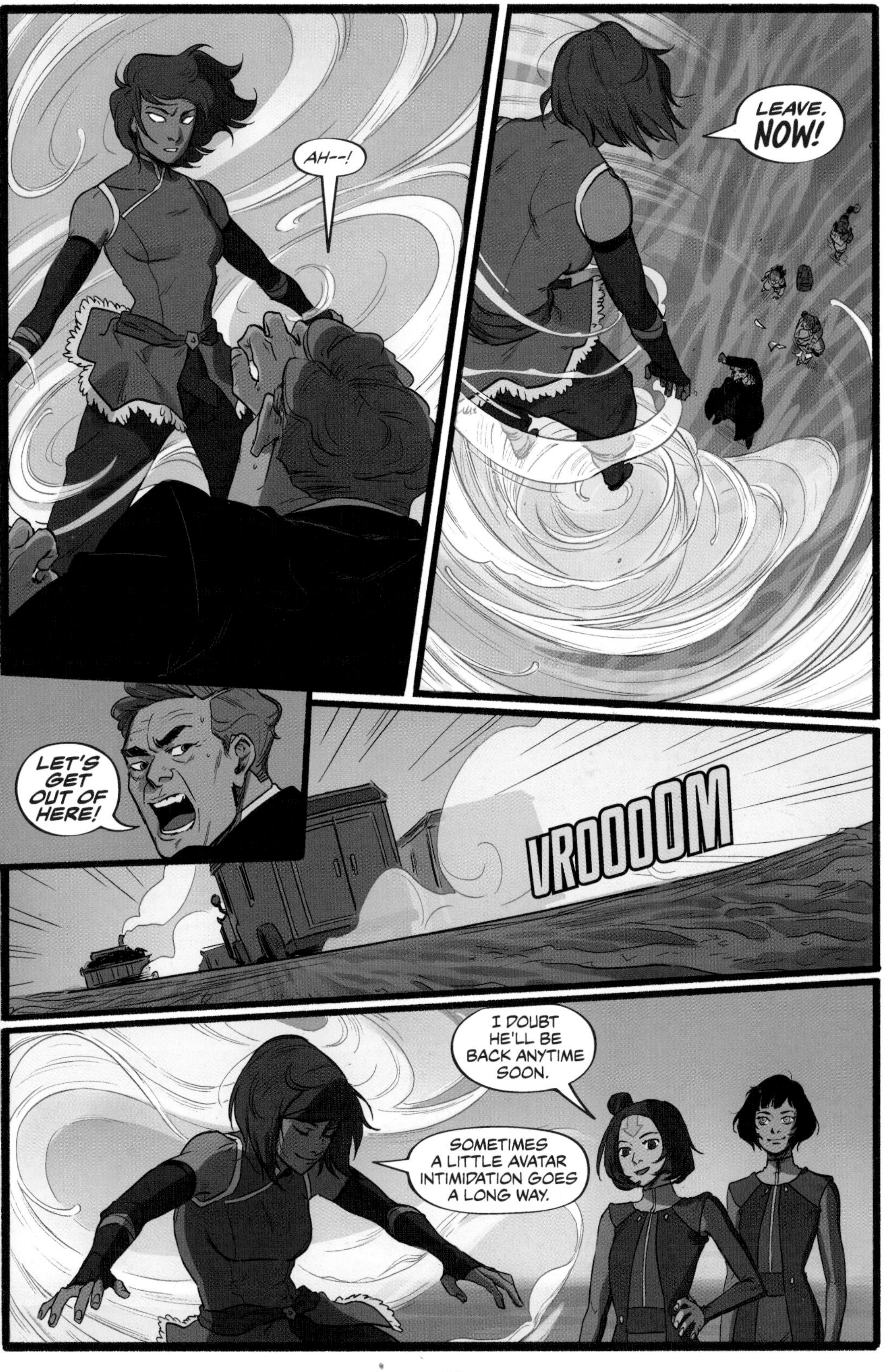
AH--!
LEAVE. NOW!
LET'S GET OUT OF HERE!
VROOOOM
I DOUBT HE'LL BE BACK ANYTIME SOON.
SOMETIMES A LITTLE AVATAR INTIMIDATION GOES A LONG WAY.

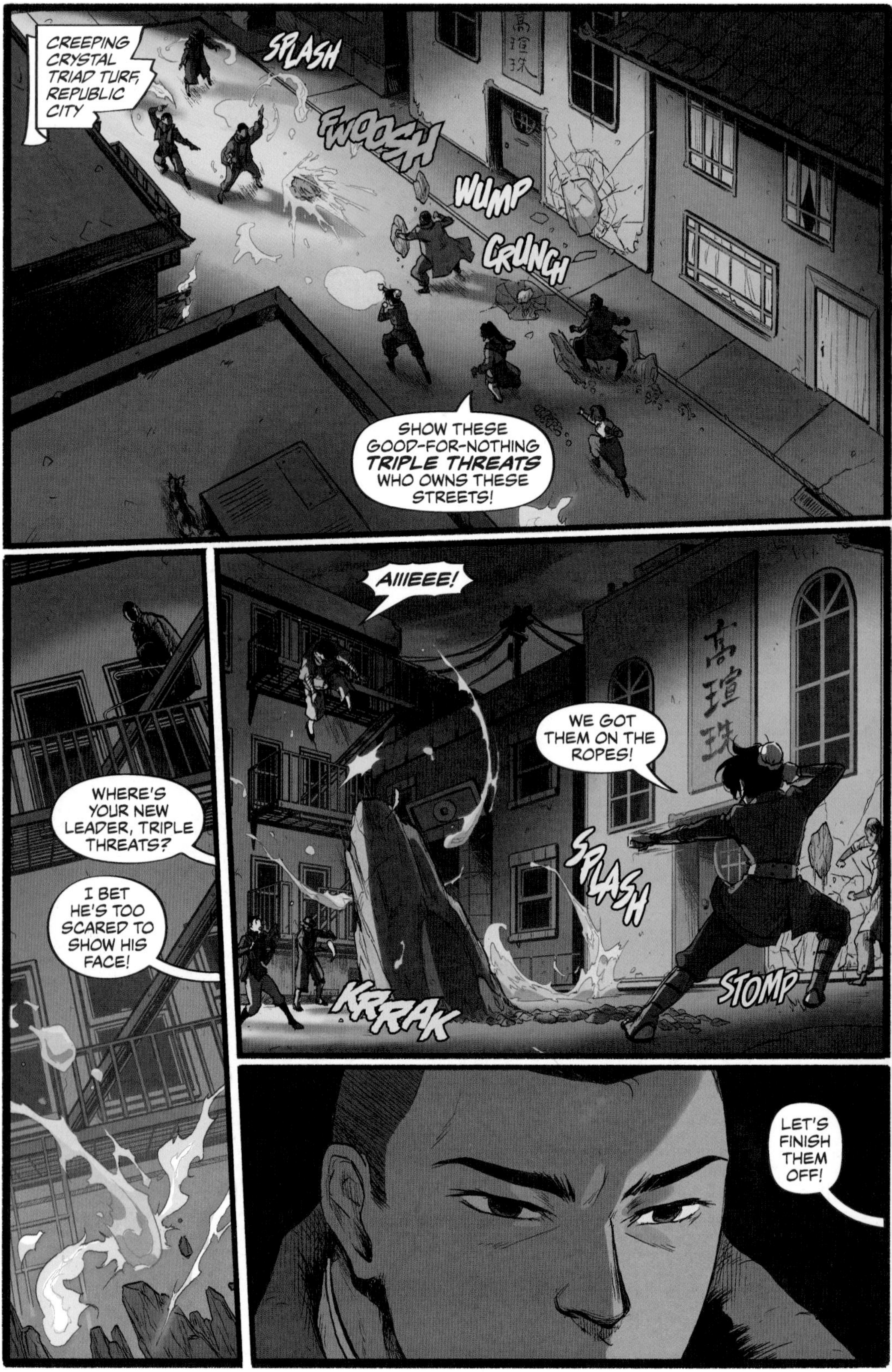
CREEPING CRYSTAL TRIAD TURF, REPUBLIC CITY
SPLASH
FWOOSH
WUMP
CRUNCH
SHOW THESE GOOD-FOR-NOTHING ***TRIPLE THREATS*** WHO OWNS THESE STREETS!
WHERE'S YOUR NEW LEADER, TRIPLE THREATS?
I BET HE'S TOO SCARED TO SHOW HIS FACE!
AIIIEEE!
WE GOT THEM ON THE ROPES!
SPLASH
KRRAK
STOMP
LET'S FINISH THEM OFF!

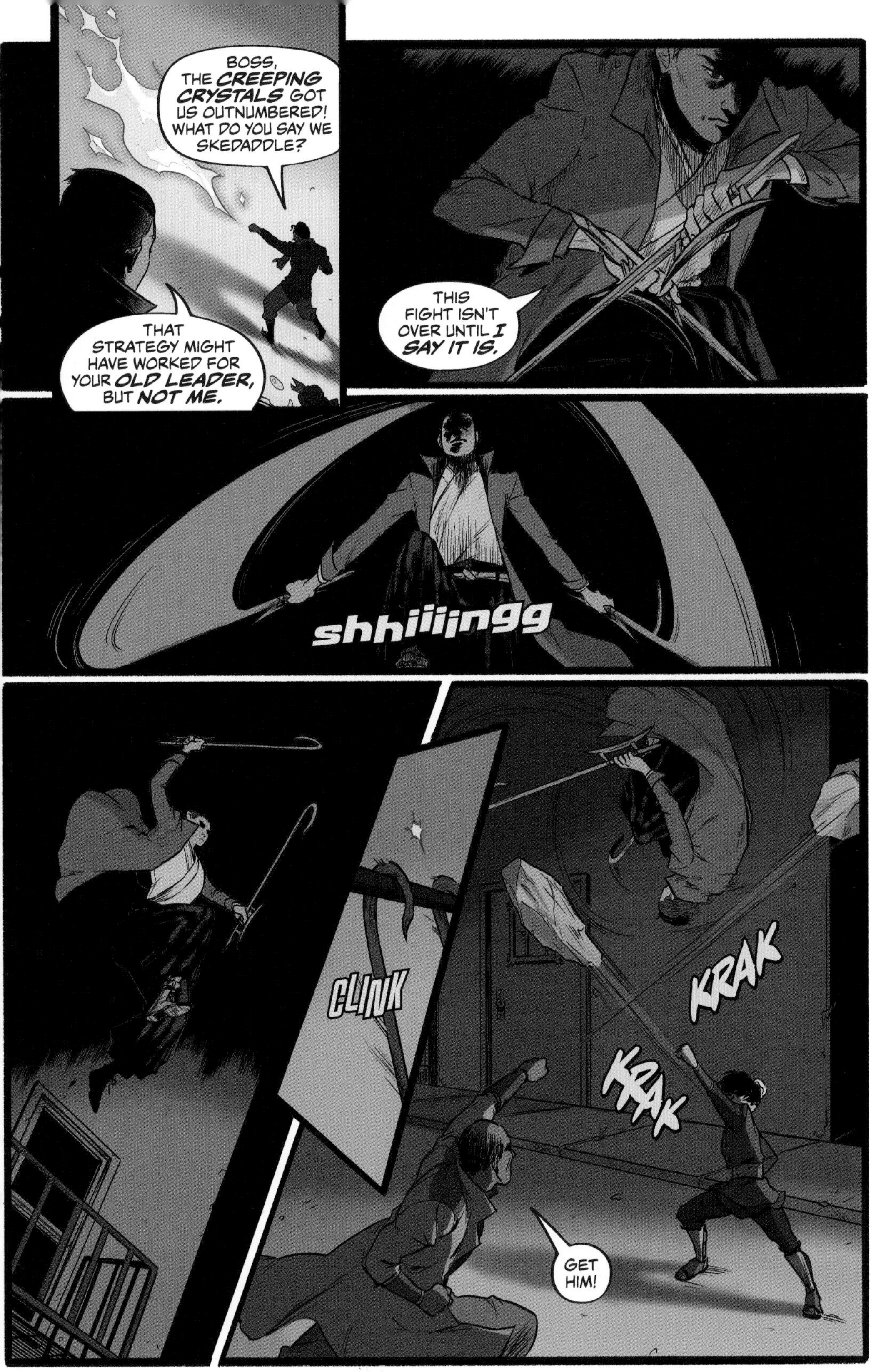

BOSS, THE CREEPING CRYSTALS GOT US OUTNUMBERED! WHAT DO YOU SAY WE SKEDADDLE?
THAT STRATEGY MIGHT HAVE WORKED FOR YOUR OLD LEADER, BUT NOT ME.
THIS FIGHT ISN'T OVER UNTIL I SAY IT IS.
shhiiiingg
CLINK
KRAK
KRAK
GET HIM!

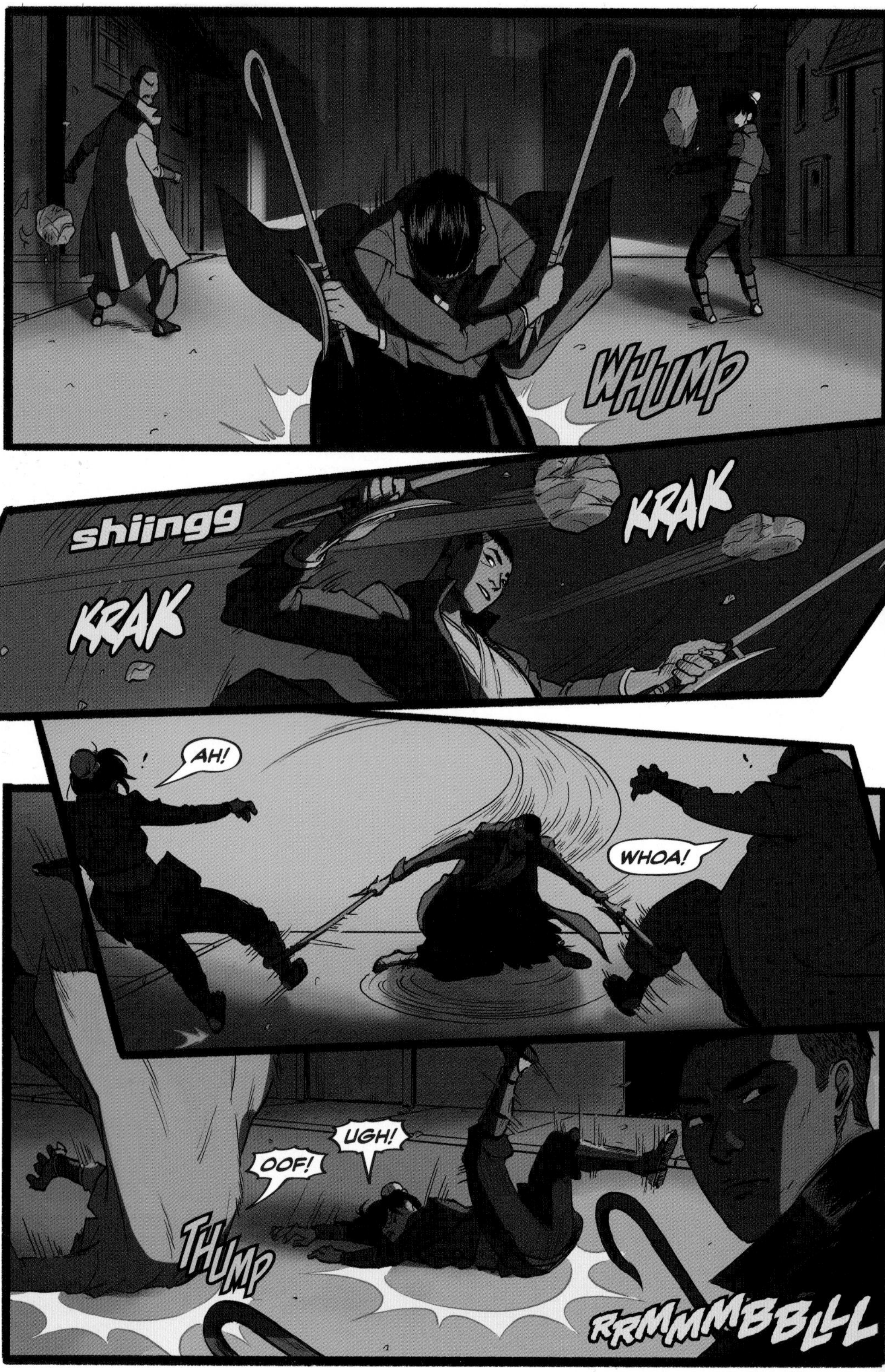
WHUMP
shiingg
KRAK
KRAK
AH!
WHOA!
UGH!
OOF!
THUMP
RRMMMMBBLLL

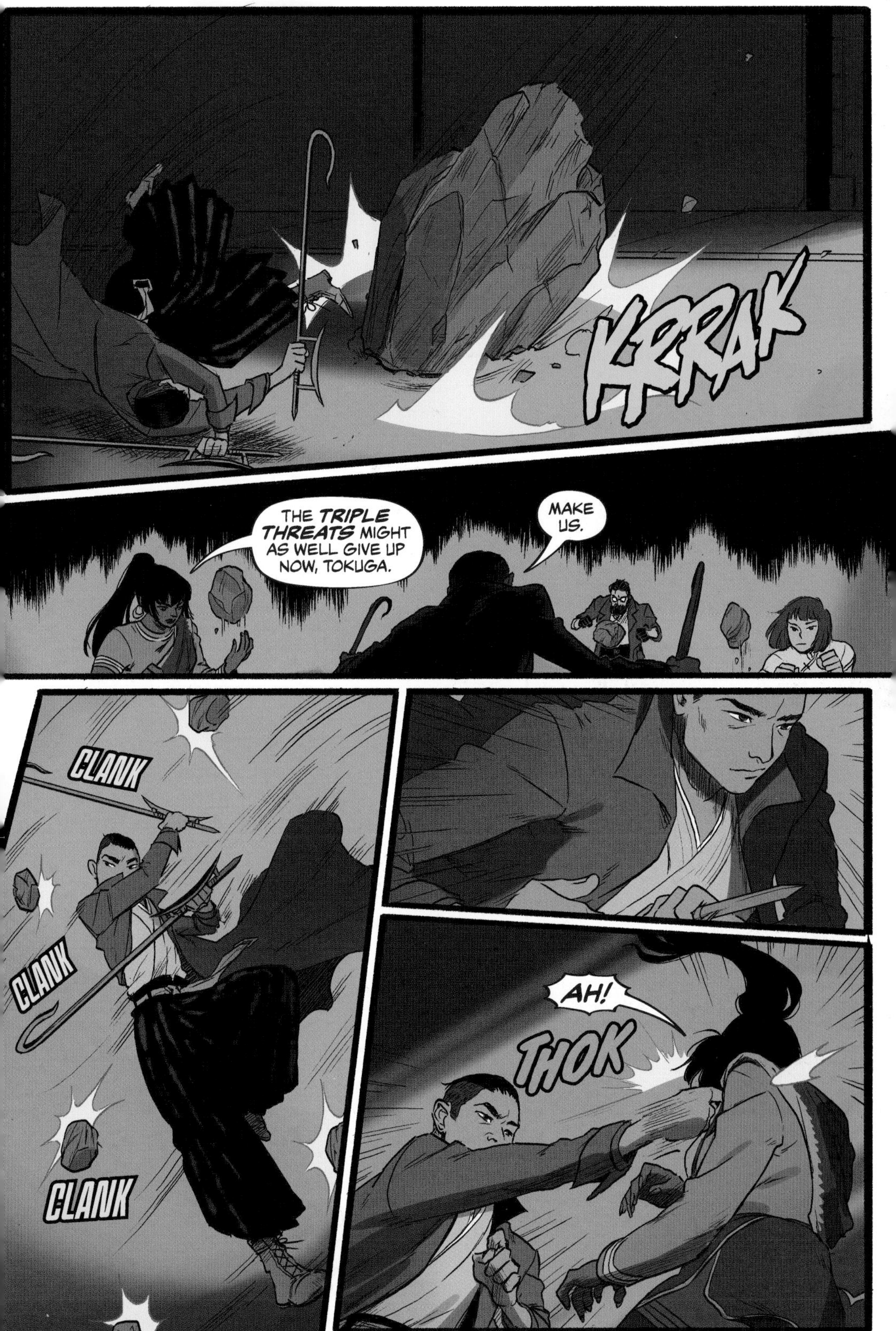
KRRAK
THE TRIPLE THREATS MIGHT AS WELL GIVE UP NOW, TOKUGA.
MAKE US.
CLANK
CLANK
CLANK
AH!
THOK

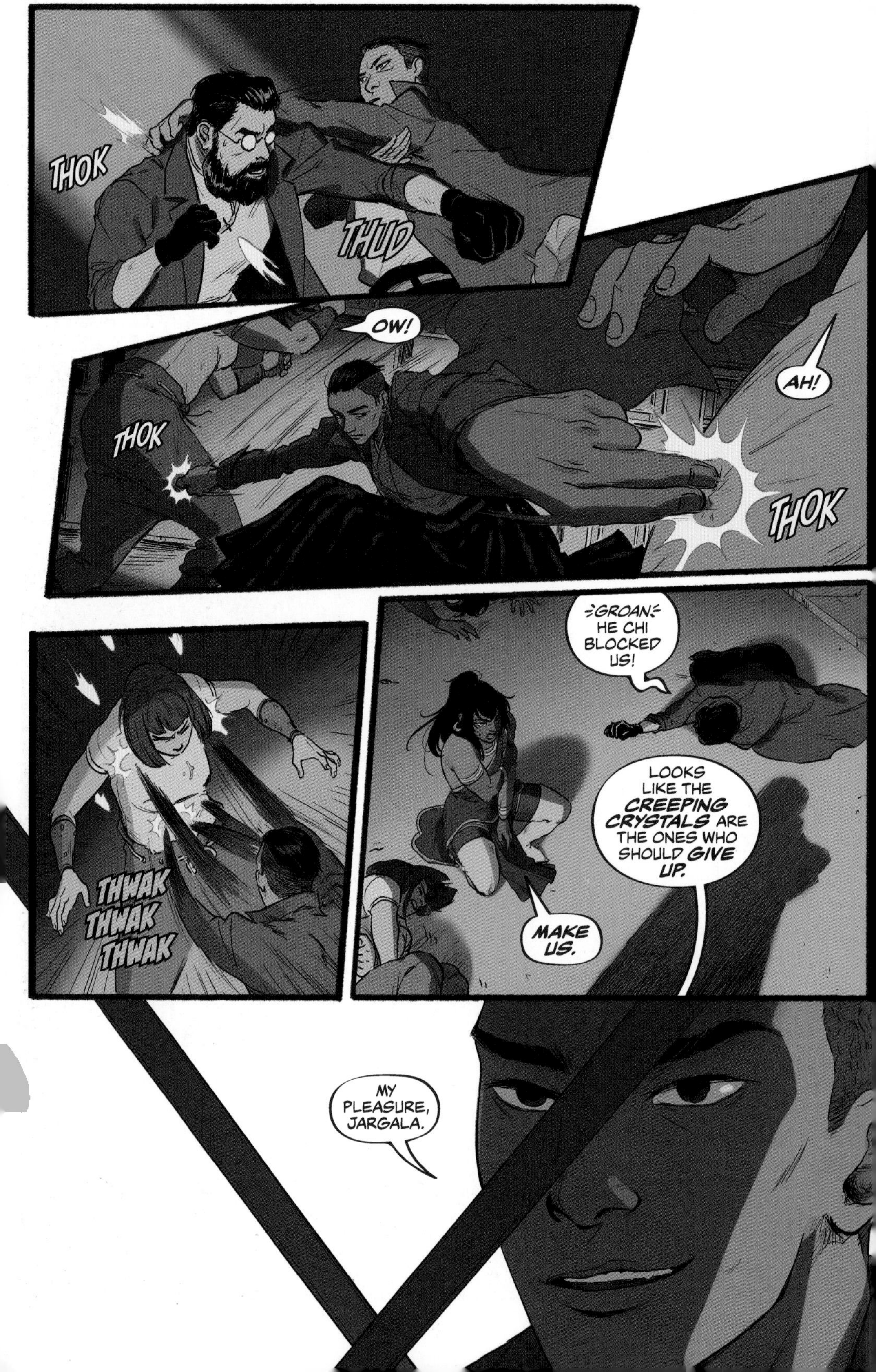
THOK
THUD
OW!
AH!
THOK
THOK
THWAK THWAK THWAK
GROAN HE CHI BLOCKED US!
LOOKS LIKE THE CREEPING CRYSTALS ARE THE ONES WHO SHOULD GIVE UP.
MAKE US.
MY PLEASURE, JARGALA.

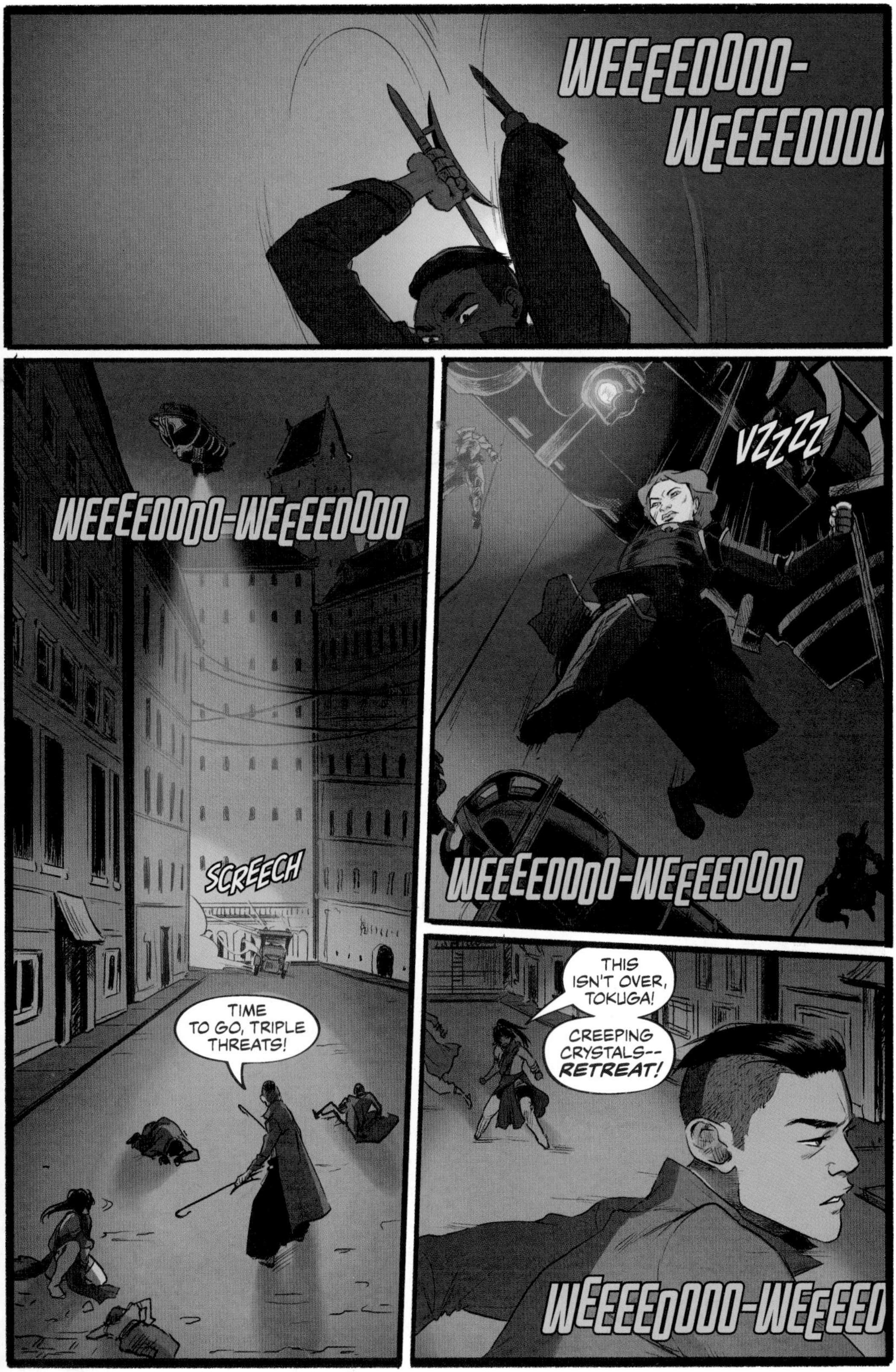
WEEEEOOOO-
WEEEEOOOO
WEEEEOOOO-WEEEEOOOO
SCREECH
TIME TO GO, TRIPLE THREATS!
VZZZZ
WEEEEOOOO-WEEEEOOOO
THIS ISN'T OVER, TOKUGA!
CREEPING CRYSTALS-- RETREAT!
WEEEEOOOO-WEEEEO

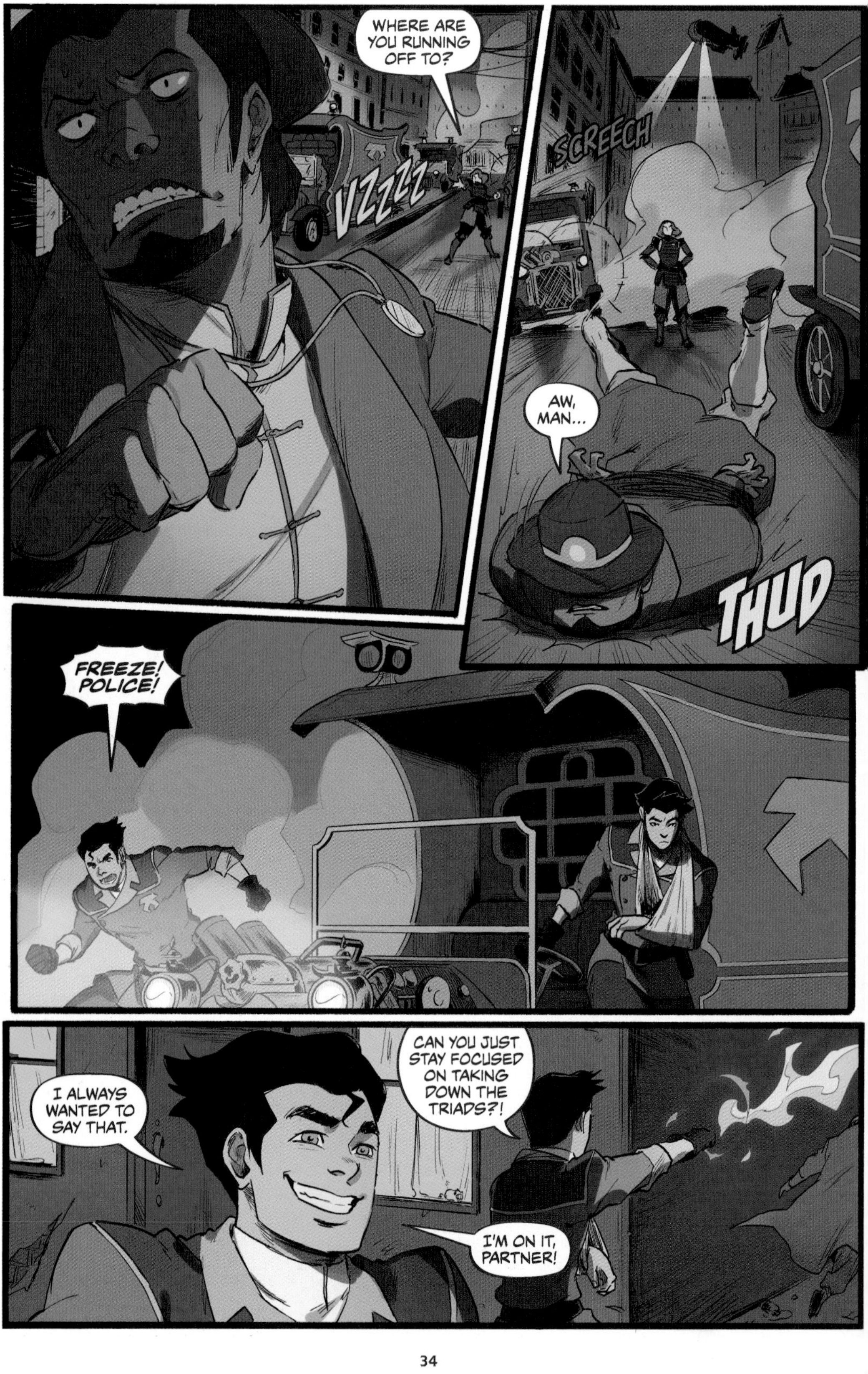
WHERE ARE YOU RUNNING OFF TO?
VZZZZ
SCREECH
AW, MAN...
THUD
FREEZE! POLICE!
I ALWAYS WANTED TO SAY THAT.
CAN YOU JUST STAY FOCUSED ON TAKING DOWN THE TRIADS?!
I'M ON IT, PARTNER!

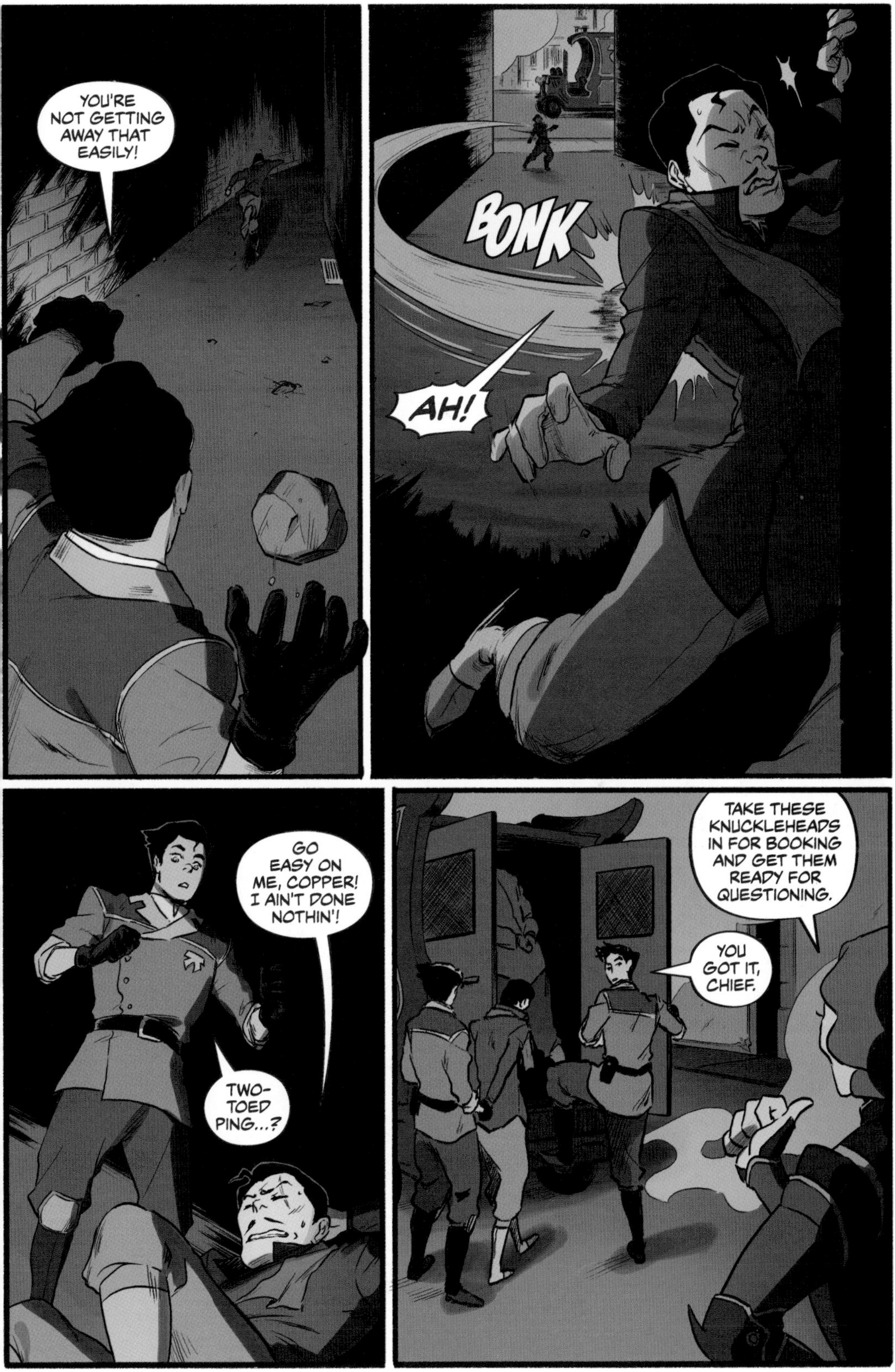
YOU'RE NOT GETTING AWAY THAT EASILY!
BONK
AH!
GO EASY ON ME, COPPER! I AIN'T DONE NOTHIN'!
TWO-TOED PING...?
TAKE THESE KNUCKLEHEADS IN FOR BOOKING AND GET THEM READY FOR QUESTIONING.
YOU GOT IT, CHIEF.

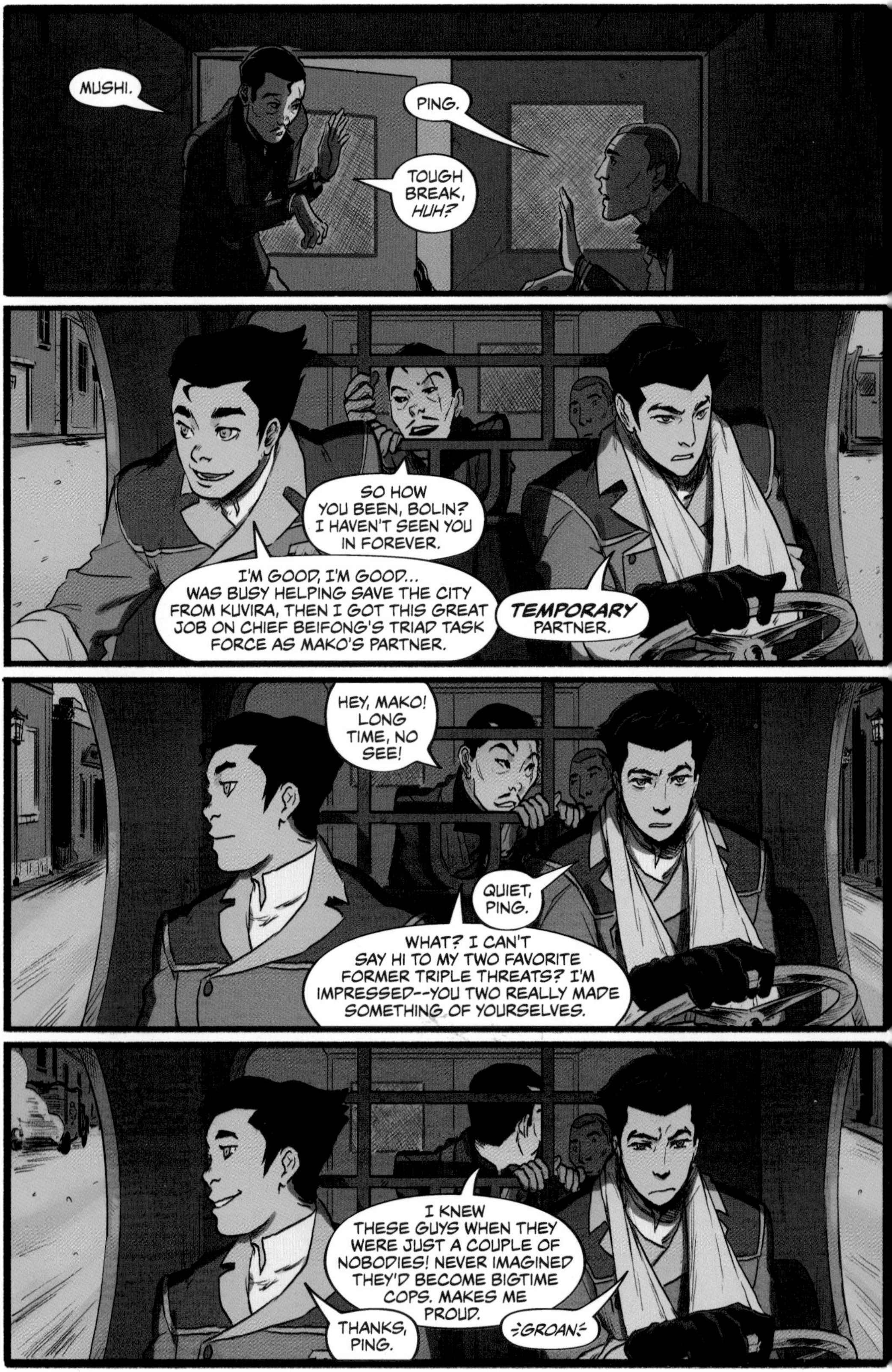
MUSHI.
PING.
TOUGH BREAK, HUH?
SO HOW YOU BEEN, BOLIN? I HAVEN'T SEEN YOU IN FOREVER.
I'M GOOD, I'M GOOD... WAS BUSY HELPING SAVE THE CITY FROM KUVIRA, THEN I GOT THIS GREAT JOB ON CHIEF BEIFONG'S TRIAD TASK FORCE AS MAKO'S PARTNER.
TEMPORARY PARTNER.
HEY, MAKO! LONG TIME, NO SEE!
QUIET, PING.
WHAT? I CAN'T SAY HI TO MY TWO FAVORITE FORMER TRIPLE THREATS? I'M IMPRESSED--YOU TWO REALLY MADE SOMETHING OF YOURSELVES.
I KNEW THESE GUYS WHEN THEY WERE JUST A COUPLE OF NOBODIES! NEVER IMAGINED THEY'D BECOME BIGTIME COPS. MAKES ME PROUD.
THANKS, PING.
GROAN

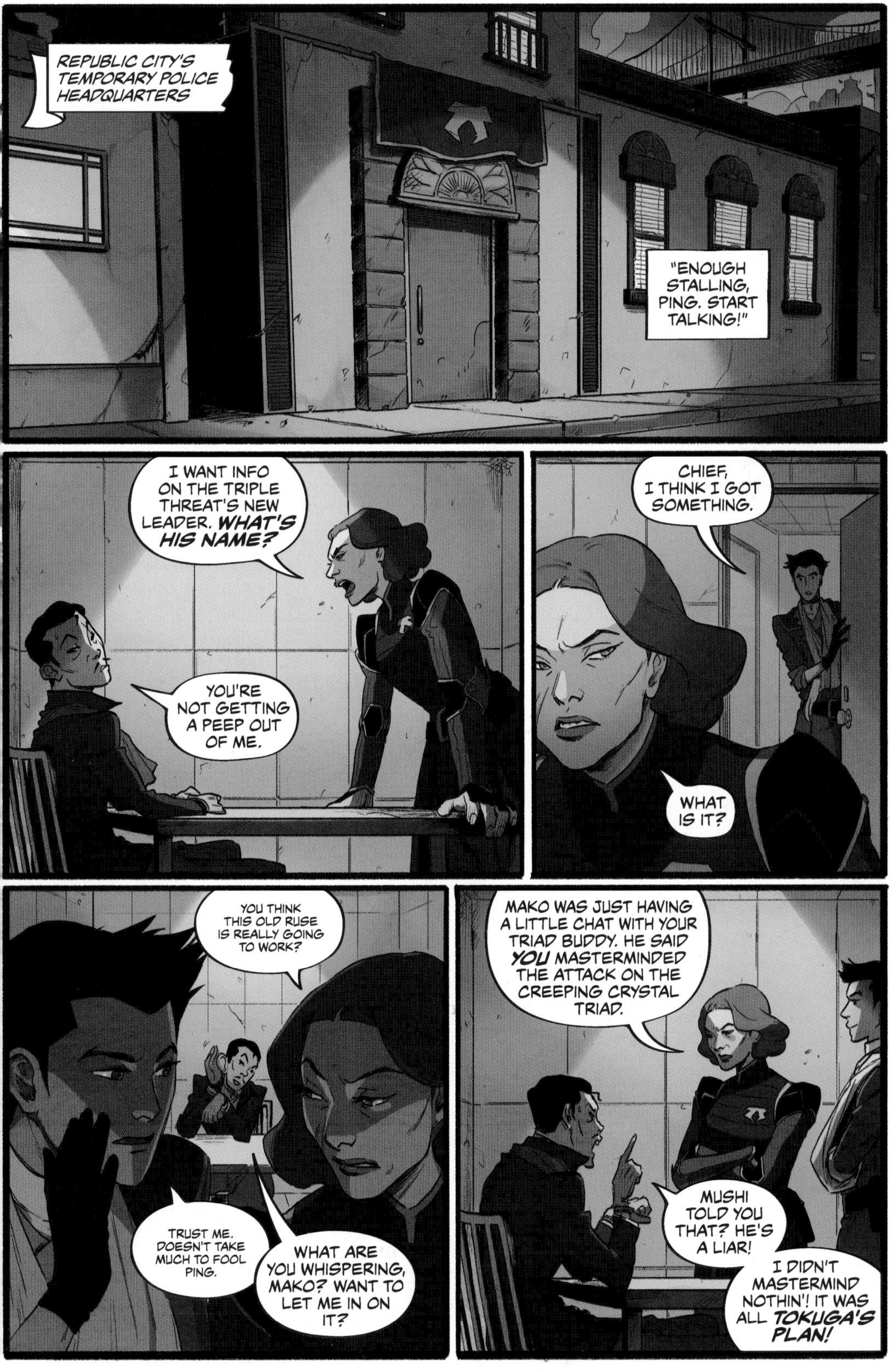
REPUBLIC CITY'S TEMPORARY POLICE HEADQUARTERS
"ENOUGH STALLING, PING. START TALKING!"
I WANT INFO ON THE TRIPLE THREAT'S NEW LEADER. WHAT'S HIS NAME?
YOU'RE NOT GETTING A PEEP OUT OF ME.
CHIEF, I THINK I GOT SOMETHING.
WHAT IS IT?
YOU THINK THIS OLD RUSE IS REALLY GOING TO WORK?
TRUST ME. DOESN'T TAKE MUCH TO FOOL PING.
WHAT ARE YOU WHISPERING, MAKO? WANT TO LET ME IN ON IT?
MAKO WAS JUST HAVING A LITTLE CHAT WITH YOUR TRIAD BUDDY. HE SAID YOU MASTERMINDED THE ATTACK ON THE CREEPING CRYSTAL TRIAD.
MUSHI TOLD YOU THAT? HE'S A LIAR!
I DIDN'T MASTERMIND NOTHIN'! IT WAS ALL TOKUGA'S PLAN!

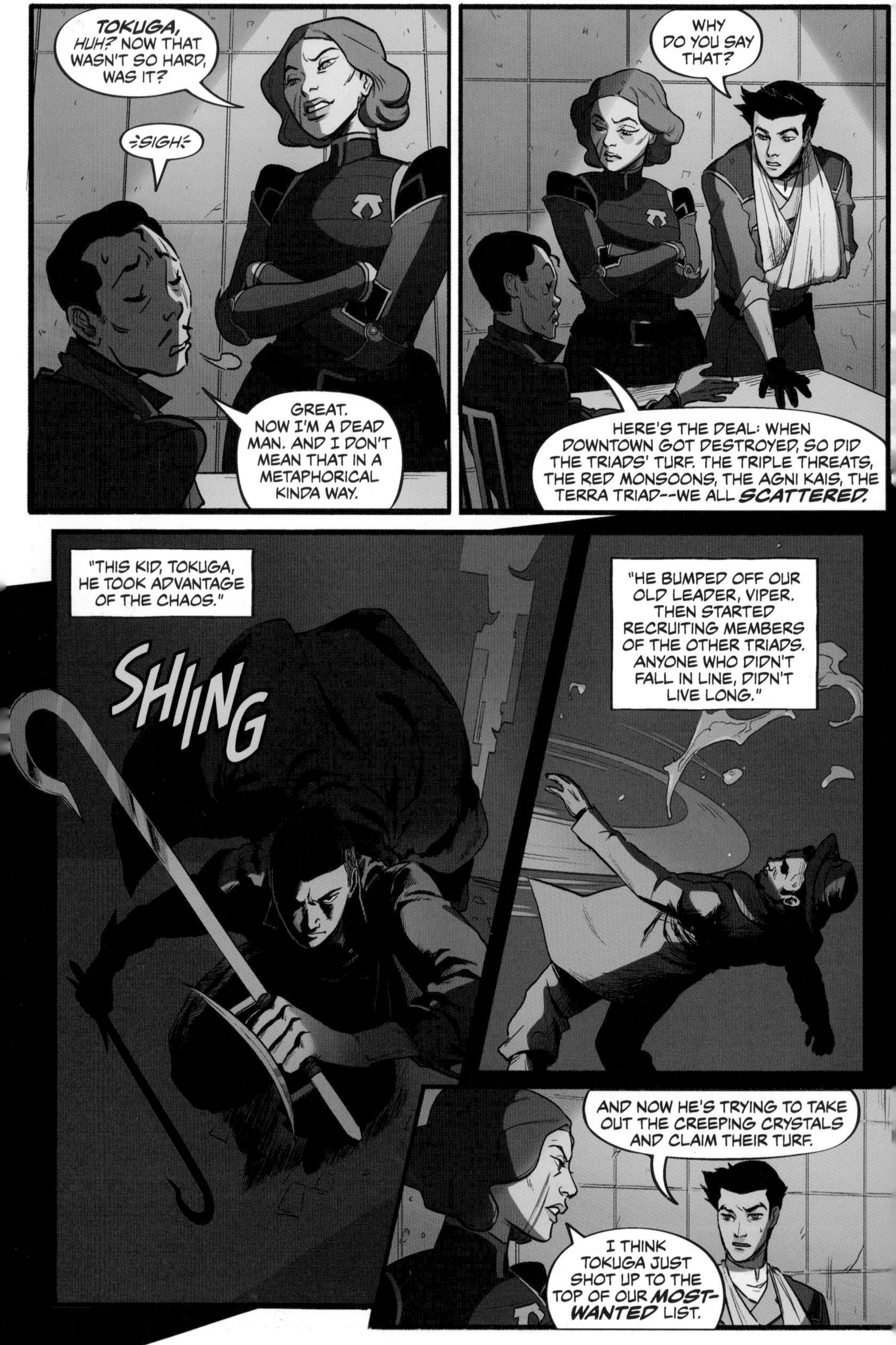
TOKUGA, HUH? NOW THAT WASN'T SO HARD, WAS IT?
:SIGH:
GREAT. NOW I'M A DEAD MAN. AND I DON'T MEAN THAT IN A METAPHORICAL KINDA WAY.
WHY DO YOU SAY THAT?
HERE'S THE DEAL: WHEN DOWNTOWN GOT DESTROYED, SO DID THE TRIADS' TURF. THE TRIPLE THREATS, THE RED MONSOONS, THE AGNI KAIS, THE TERRA TRIAD--WE ALL SCATTERED.
"THIS KID, TOKUGA, HE TOOK ADVANTAGE OF THE CHAOS."
SHIIING
"HE BUMPED OFF OUR OLD LEADER, VIPER. THEN STARTED RECRUITING MEMBERS OF THE OTHER TRIADS. ANYONE WHO DIDN'T FALL IN LINE, DIDN'T LIVE LONG."
AND NOW HE'S TRYING TO TAKE OUT THE CREEPING CRYSTALS AND CLAIM THEIR TURF.
I THINK TOKUGA JUST SHOT UP TO THE TOP OF OUR MOST-WANTED LIST.

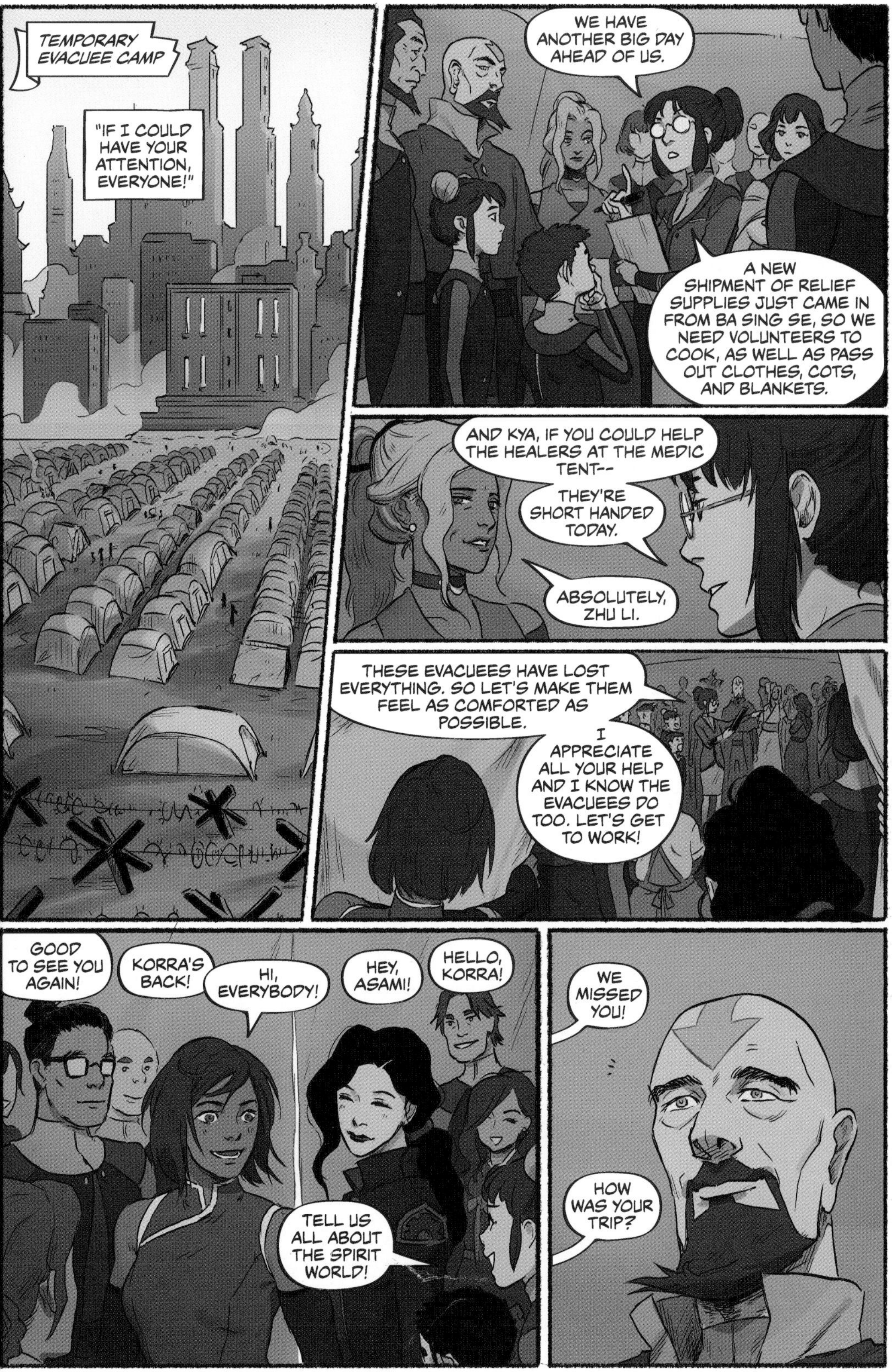
TEMPORARY EVACUEE CAMP
"IF I COULD HAVE YOUR ATTENTION, EVERYONE!"
WE HAVE ANOTHER BIG DAY AHEAD OF US.
A NEW SHIPMENT OF RELIEF SUPPLIES JUST CAME IN FROM BA SING SE, SO WE NEED VOLUNTEERS TO COOK, AS WELL AS PASS OUT CLOTHES, COTS, AND BLANKETS.
AND KYA, IF YOU COULD HELP THE HEALERS AT THE MEDIC TENT--
THEY'RE SHORT HANDED TODAY.
ABSOLUTELY, ZHU LI.
THESE EVACUEES HAVE LOST EVERYTHING. SO LET'S MAKE THEM FEEL AS COMFORTED AS POSSIBLE.
I APPRECIATE ALL YOUR HELP AND I KNOW THE EVACUEES DO TOO. LET'S GET TO WORK!
GOOD TO SEE YOU AGAIN!
KORRA'S BACK!
HI, EVERYBODY!
HEY, ASAMI!
HELLO, KORRA!
TELL US ALL ABOUT THE SPIRIT WORLD!
WE MISSED YOU!
HOW WAS YOUR TRIP?

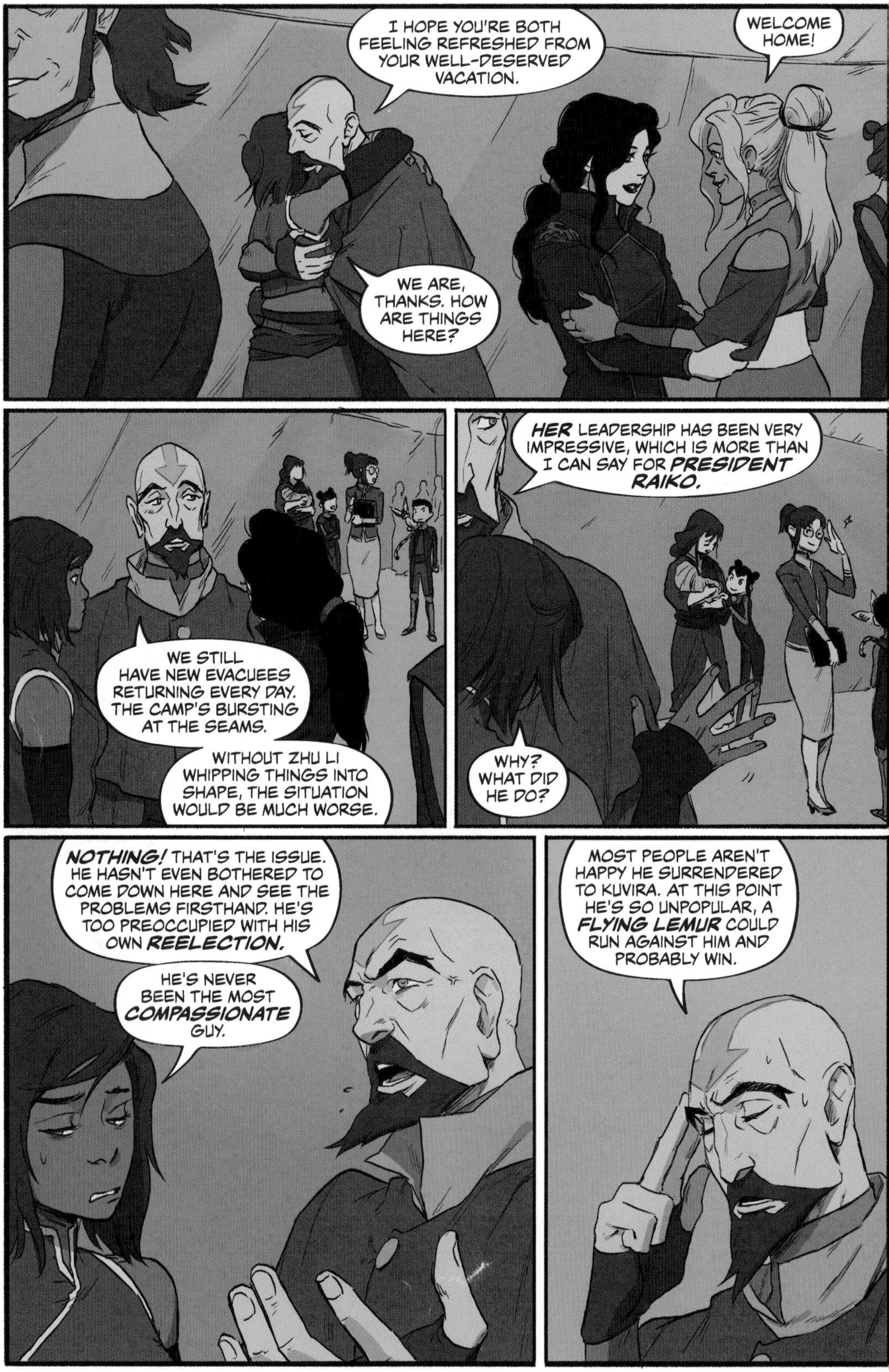
I HOPE YOU'RE BOTH FEELING REFRESHED FROM YOUR WELL-DESERVED VACATION.
WELCOME HOME!
WE ARE, THANKS. HOW ARE THINGS HERE?
WE STILL HAVE NEW EVACUEES RETURNING EVERY DAY. THE CAMP'S BURSTING AT THE SEAMS.
WITHOUT ZHU LI WHIPPING THINGS INTO SHAPE, THE SITUATION WOULD BE MUCH WORSE.
HER LEADERSHIP HAS BEEN VERY IMPRESSIVE, WHICH IS MORE THAN I CAN SAY FOR PRESIDENT RAIKO.
WHY? WHAT DID HE DO?
NOTHING! THAT'S THE ISSUE. HE HASN'T EVEN BOTHERED TO COME DOWN HERE AND SEE THE PROBLEMS FIRSTHAND. HE'S TOO PREOCCUPIED WITH HIS OWN REELECTION.
HE'S NEVER BEEN THE MOST COMPASSIONATE GUY.
MOST PEOPLE AREN'T HAPPY HE SURRENDERED TO KUVIRA. AT THIS POINT HE'S SO UNPOPULAR, A FLYING LEMUR COULD RUN AGAINST HIM AND PROBABLY WIN.

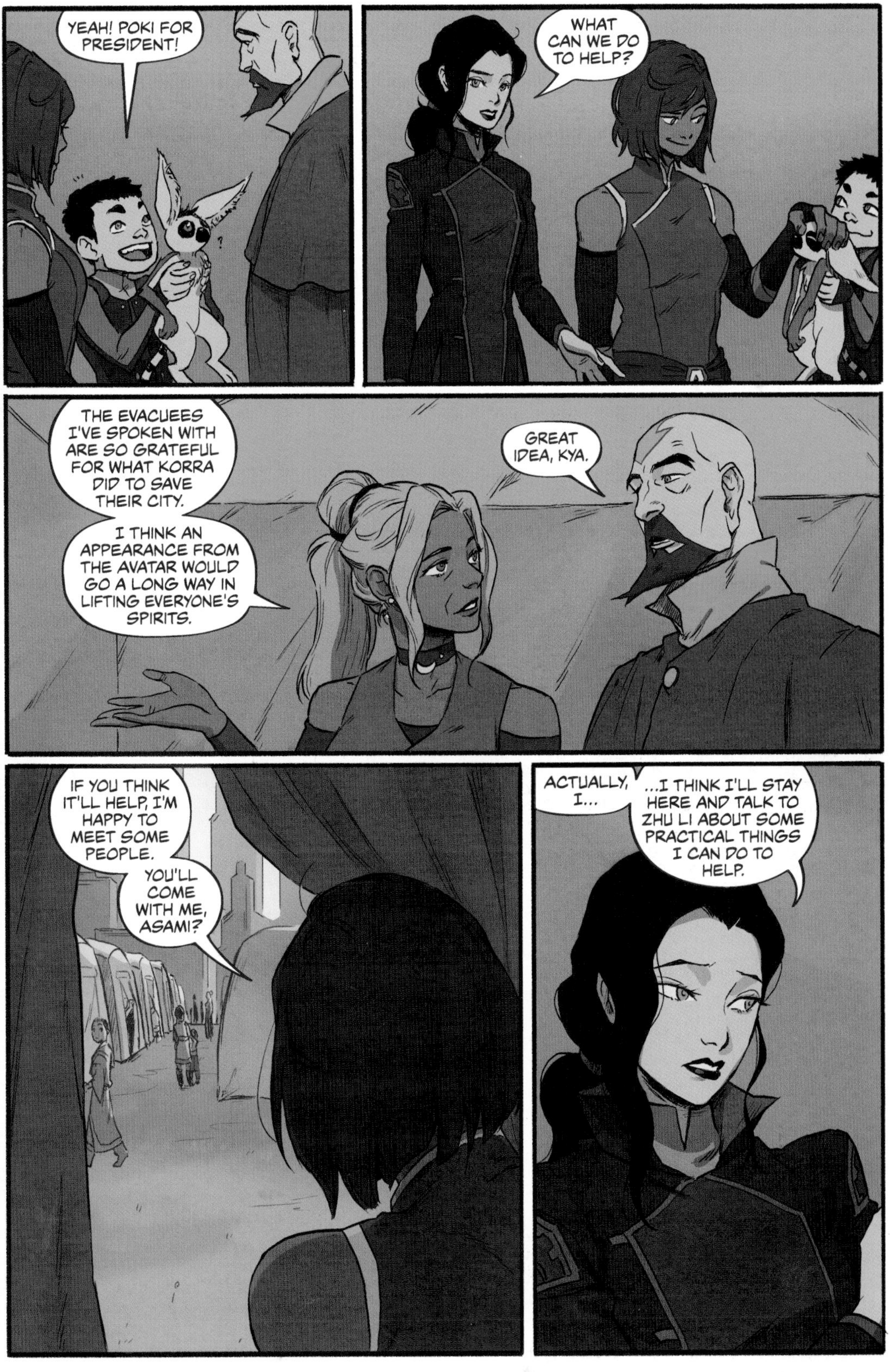
YEAH! POKI FOR PRESIDENT!
WHAT CAN WE DO TO HELP?
THE EVACUEES I'VE SPOKEN WITH ARE SO GRATEFUL FOR WHAT KORRA DID TO SAVE THEIR CITY.
I THINK AN APPEARANCE FROM THE AVATAR WOULD GO A LONG WAY IN LIFTING EVERYONE'S SPIRITS.
GREAT IDEA, KYA.
IF YOU THINK IT'LL HELP, I'M HAPPY TO MEET SOME PEOPLE.
YOU'LL COME WITH ME, ASAMI?
ACTUALLY, I...
...I THINK I'LL STAY HERE AND TALK TO ZHU LI ABOUT SOME PRACTICAL THINGS I CAN DO TO HELP.

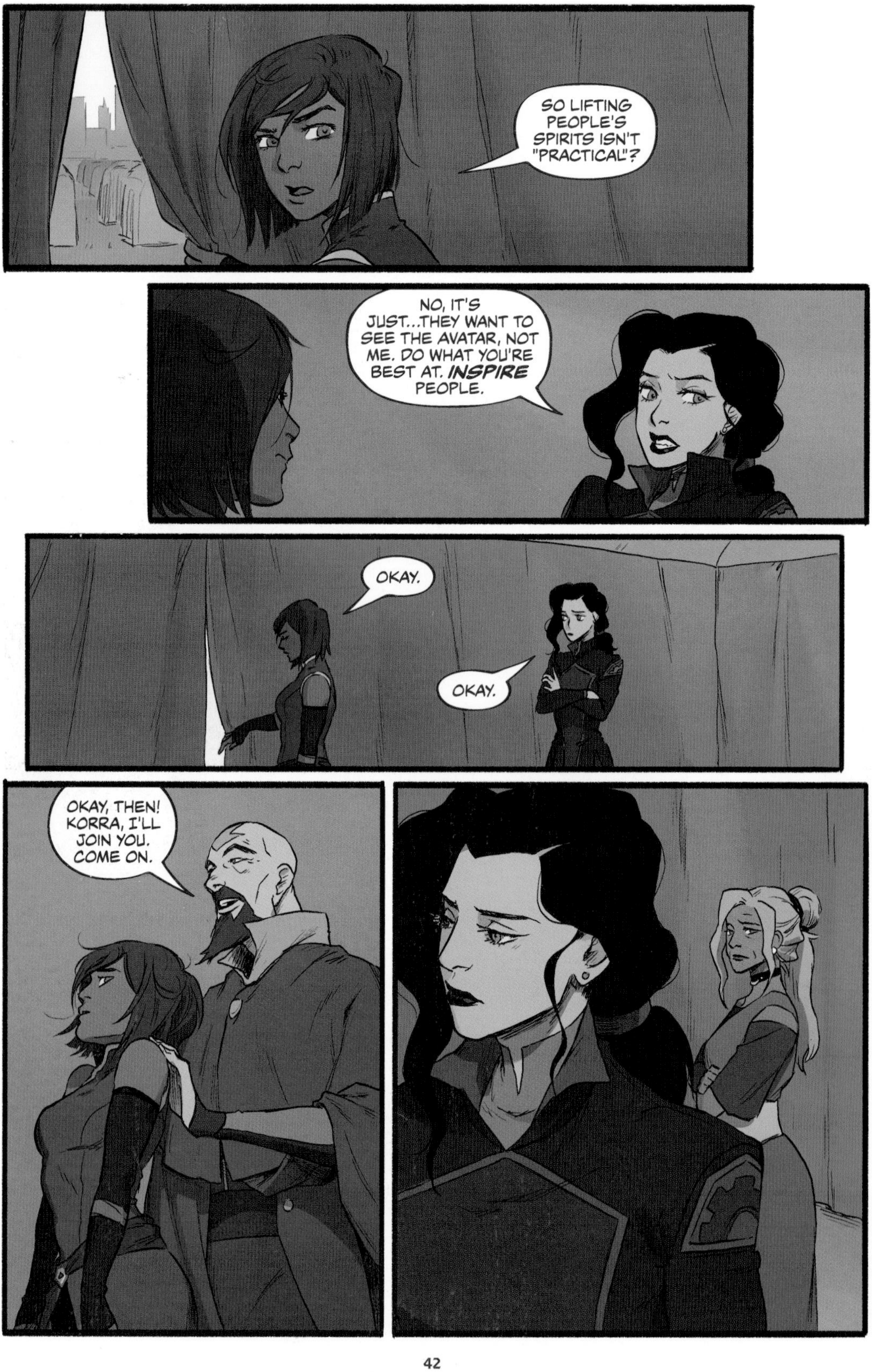
SO LIFTING PEOPLE'S SPIRITS ISN'T "PRACTICAL"?
NO, IT'S JUST...THEY WANT TO SEE THE AVATAR, NOT ME. DO WHAT YOU'RE BEST AT. *INSPIRE* PEOPLE.
OKAY.
OKAY.
OKAY, THEN! KORRA, I'LL JOIN YOU. COME ON.

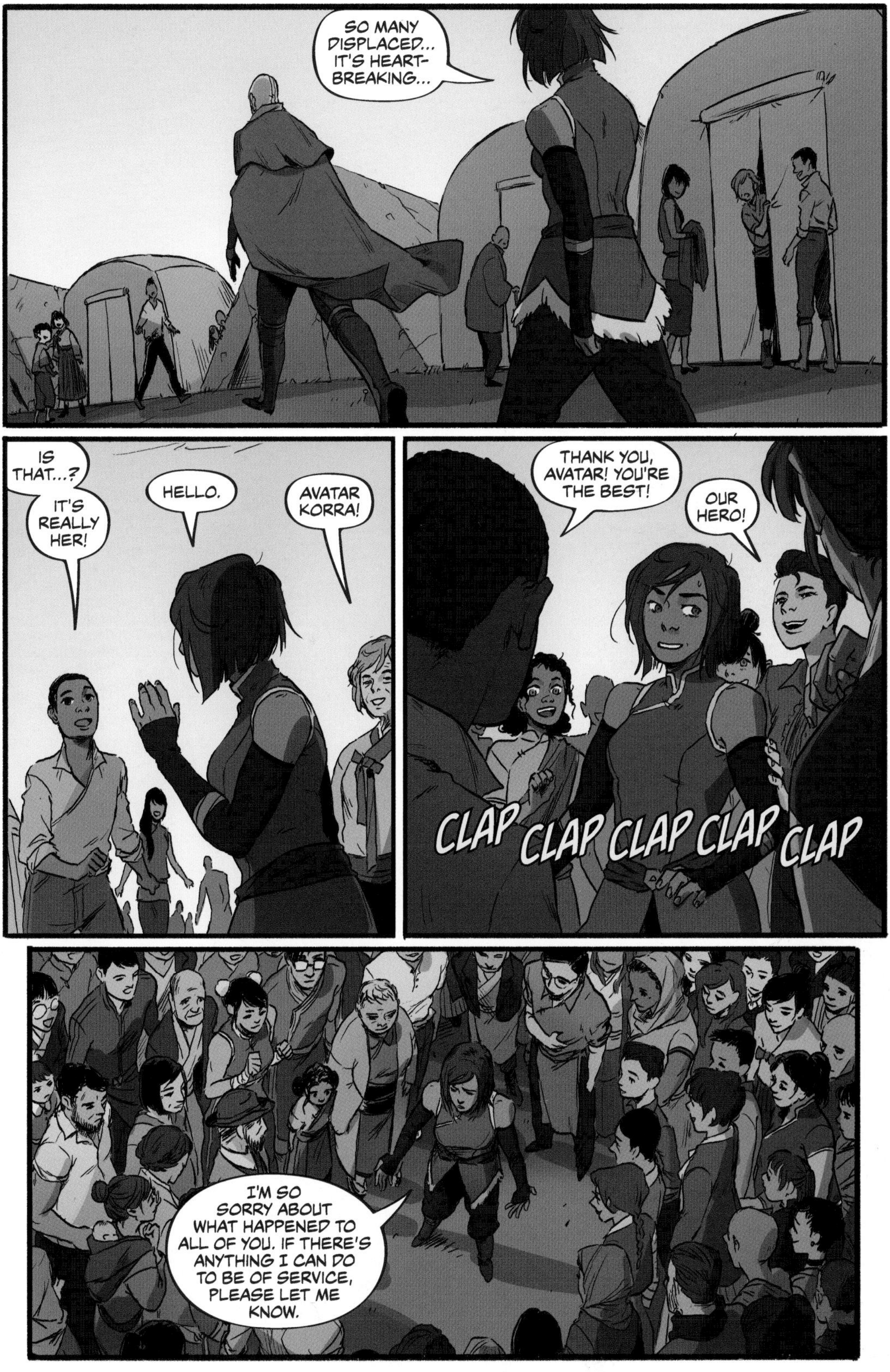
SO MANY DISPLACED... IT'S HEART-BREAKING...
IS THAT...?
IT'S REALLY HER!
HELLO.
AVATAR KORRA!
THANK YOU, AVATAR! YOU'RE THE BEST!
OUR HERO!
CLAP CLAP CLAP CLAP CLAP
I'M SO SORRY ABOUT WHAT HAPPENED TO ALL OF YOU. IF THERE'S ANYTHING I CAN DO TO BE OF SERVICE, PLEASE LET ME KNOW.

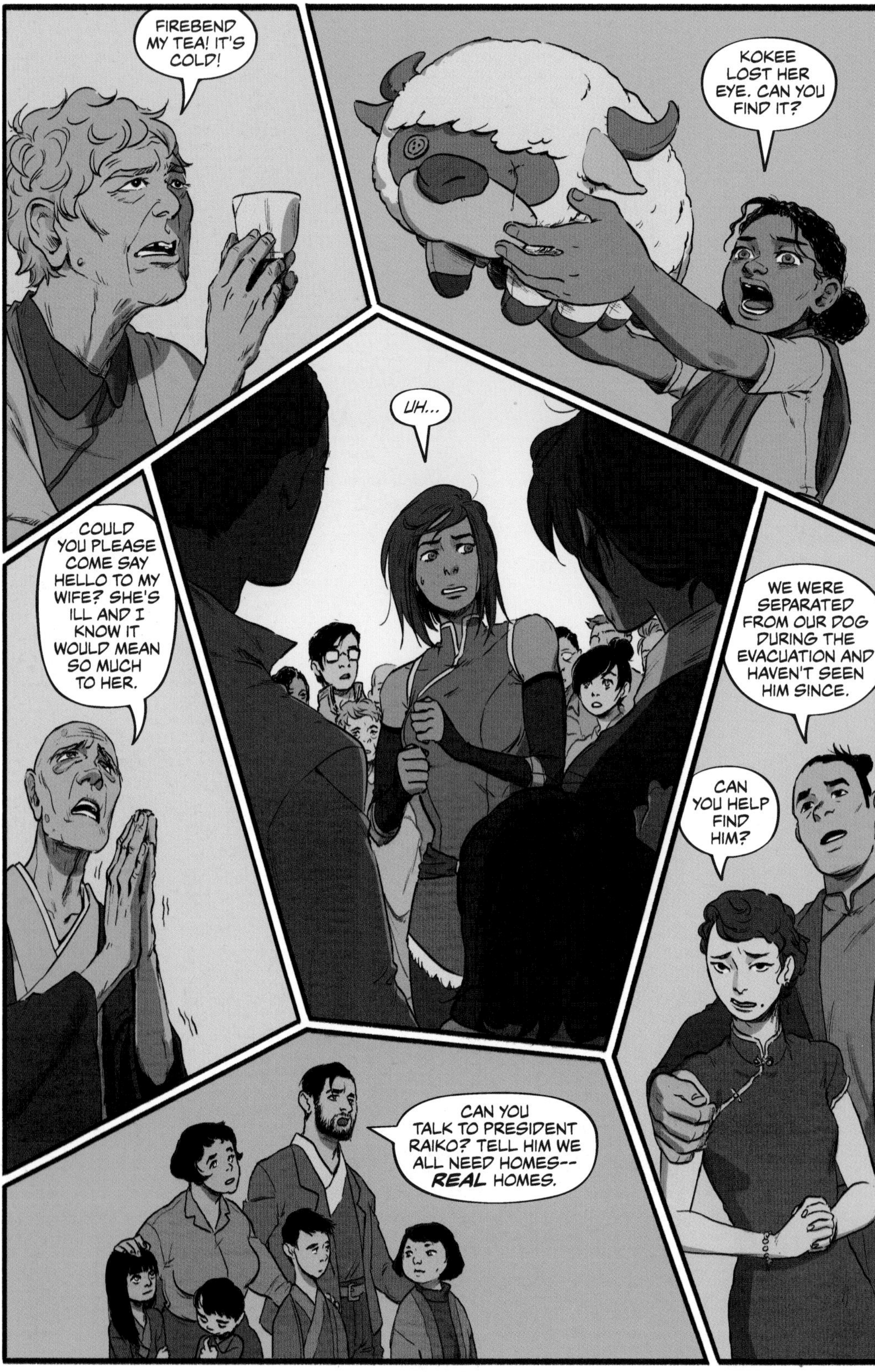
FIREBEND MY TEA! IT'S COLD!
KOKEE LOST HER EYE. CAN YOU FIND IT?
UH...
COULD YOU PLEASE COME SAY HELLO TO MY WIFE? SHE'S ILL AND I KNOW IT WOULD MEAN SO MUCH TO HER.
WE WERE SEPARATED FROM OUR DOG DURING THE EVACUATION AND HAVEN'T SEEN HIM SINCE.
CAN YOU HELP FIND HIM?
CAN YOU TALK TO PRESIDENT RAIKO? TELL HIM WE ALL NEED HOMES-- ***REAL*** HOMES.

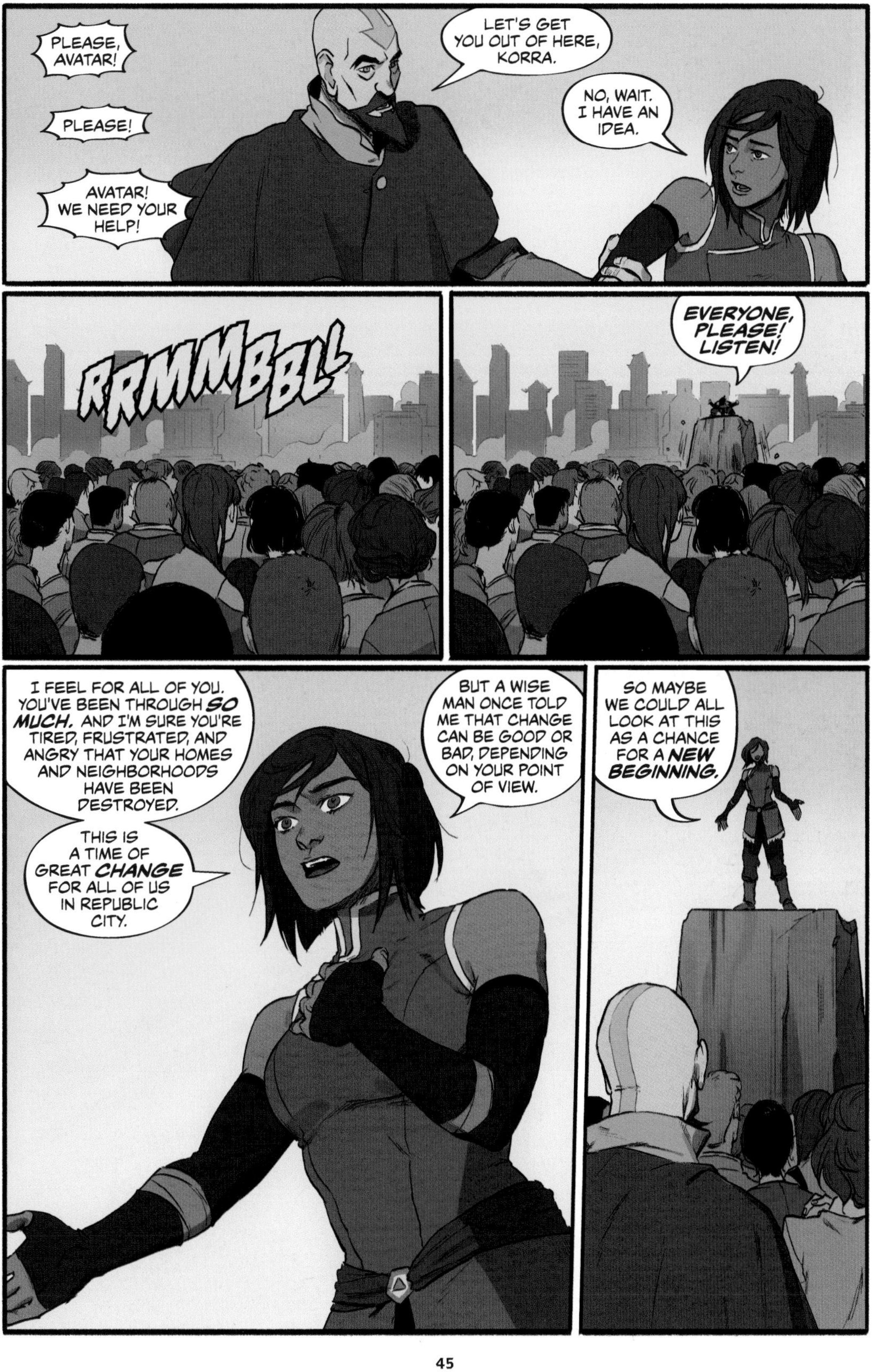
PLEASE, AVATAR!
PLEASE!
AVATAR! WE NEED YOUR HELP!
LET'S GET YOU OUT OF HERE, KORRA.
NO, WAIT. I HAVE AN IDEA.
RRMMBBLL
EVERYONE, PLEASE! LISTEN!
I FEEL FOR ALL OF YOU. YOU'VE BEEN THROUGH SO MUCH. AND I'M SURE YOU'RE TIRED, FRUSTRATED, AND ANGRY THAT YOUR HOMES AND NEIGHBORHOODS HAVE BEEN DESTROYED.
THIS IS A TIME OF GREAT CHANGE FOR ALL OF US IN REPUBLIC CITY.
BUT A WISE MAN ONCE TOLD ME THAT CHANGE CAN BE GOOD OR BAD, DEPENDING ON YOUR POINT OF VIEW.
SO MAYBE WE COULD ALL LOOK AT THIS AS A CHANCE FOR A NEW BEGINNING.

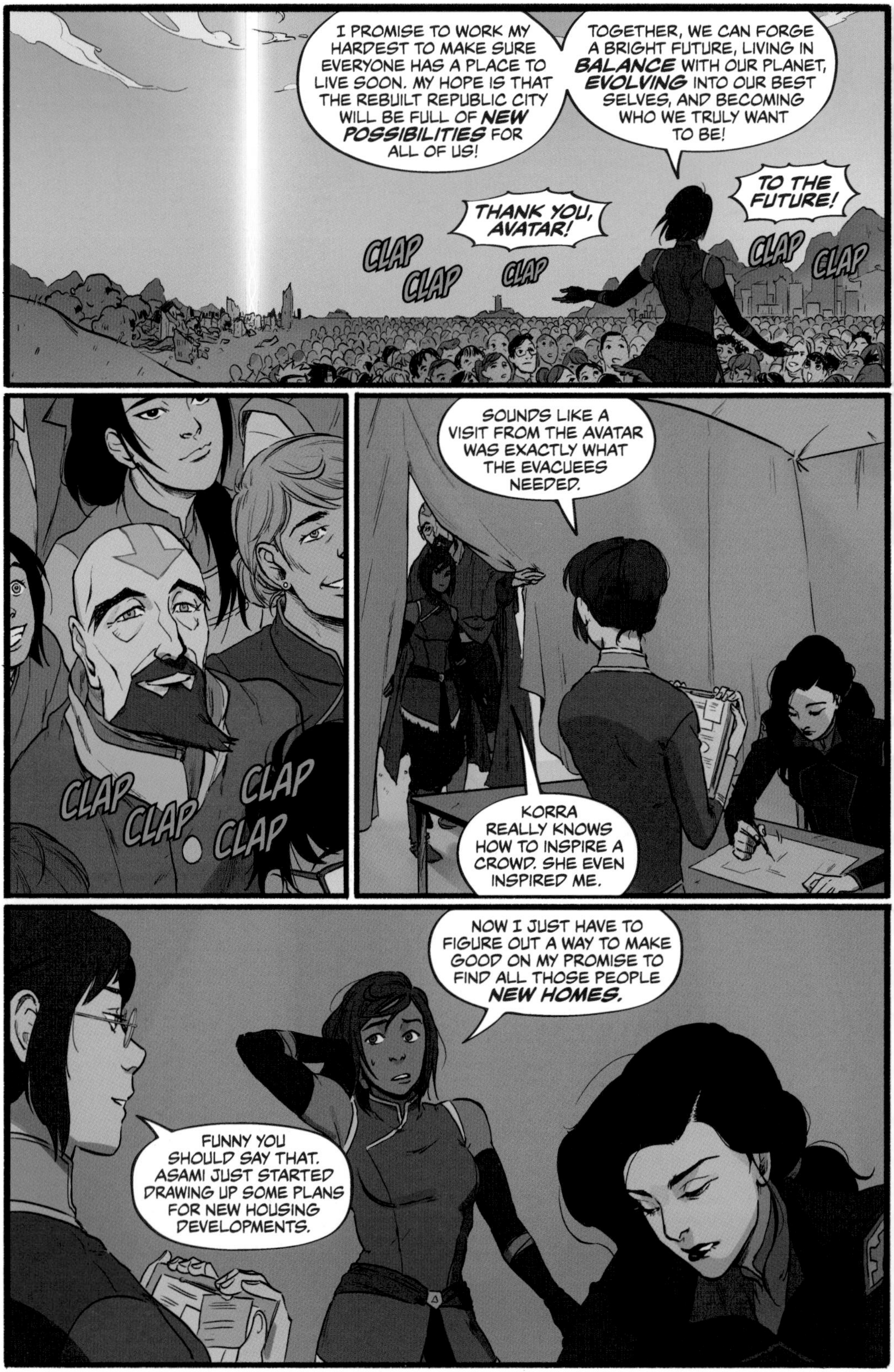
I PROMISE TO WORK MY HARDEST TO MAKE SURE EVERYONE HAS A PLACE TO LIVE SOON. MY HOPE IS THAT THE REBUILT REPUBLIC CITY WILL BE FULL OF **NEW POSSIBILITIES** FOR ALL OF US!
TOGETHER, WE CAN FORGE A BRIGHT FUTURE, LIVING IN **BALANCE** WITH OUR PLANET, **EVOLVING** INTO OUR BEST SELVES, AND BECOMING WHO WE TRULY WANT TO BE!
THANK YOU, AVATAR!
TO THE FUTURE!
CLAP
CLAP
CLAP
CLAP
CLAP
CLAP
CLAP
CLAP
CLAP
SOUNDS LIKE A VISIT FROM THE AVATAR WAS EXACTLY WHAT THE EVACUEES NEEDED.
KORRA REALLY KNOWS HOW TO INSPIRE A CROWD. SHE EVEN INSPIRED ME.
NOW I JUST HAVE TO FIGURE OUT A WAY TO MAKE GOOD ON MY PROMISE TO FIND ALL THOSE PEOPLE **NEW HOMES.**
FUNNY YOU SHOULD SAY THAT. ASAMI JUST STARTED DRAWING UP SOME PLANS FOR NEW HOUSING DEVELOPMENTS.

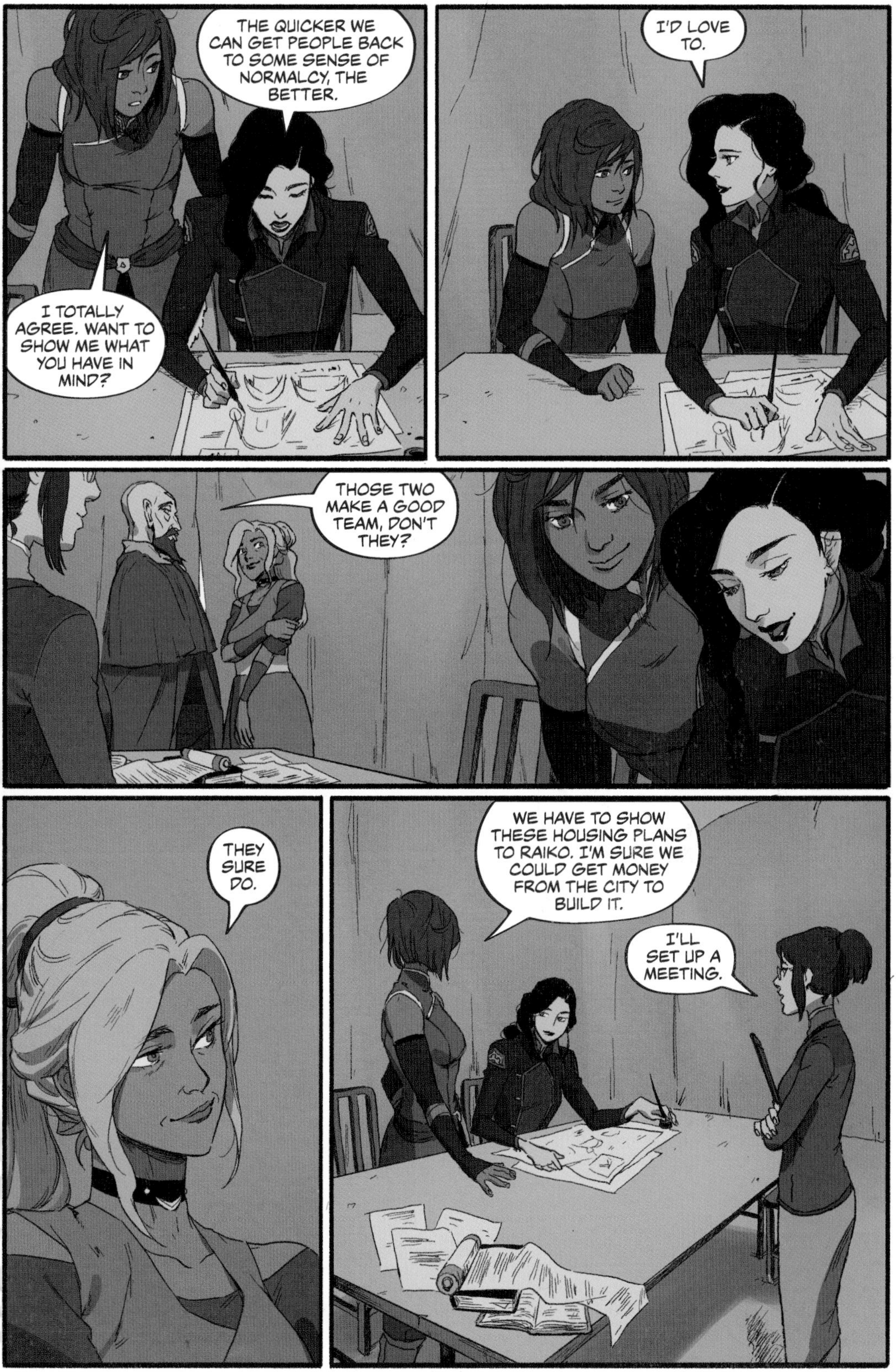
THE QUICKER WE CAN GET PEOPLE BACK TO SOME SENSE OF NORMALCY, THE BETTER.
I TOTALLY AGREE. WANT TO SHOW ME WHAT YOU HAVE IN MIND?
I'D LOVE TO.
THOSE TWO MAKE A GOOD TEAM, DON'T THEY?
THEY SURE DO.
WE HAVE TO SHOW THESE HOUSING PLANS TO RAIKO. I'M SURE WE COULD GET MONEY FROM THE CITY TO BUILD IT.
I'LL SET UP A MEETING.

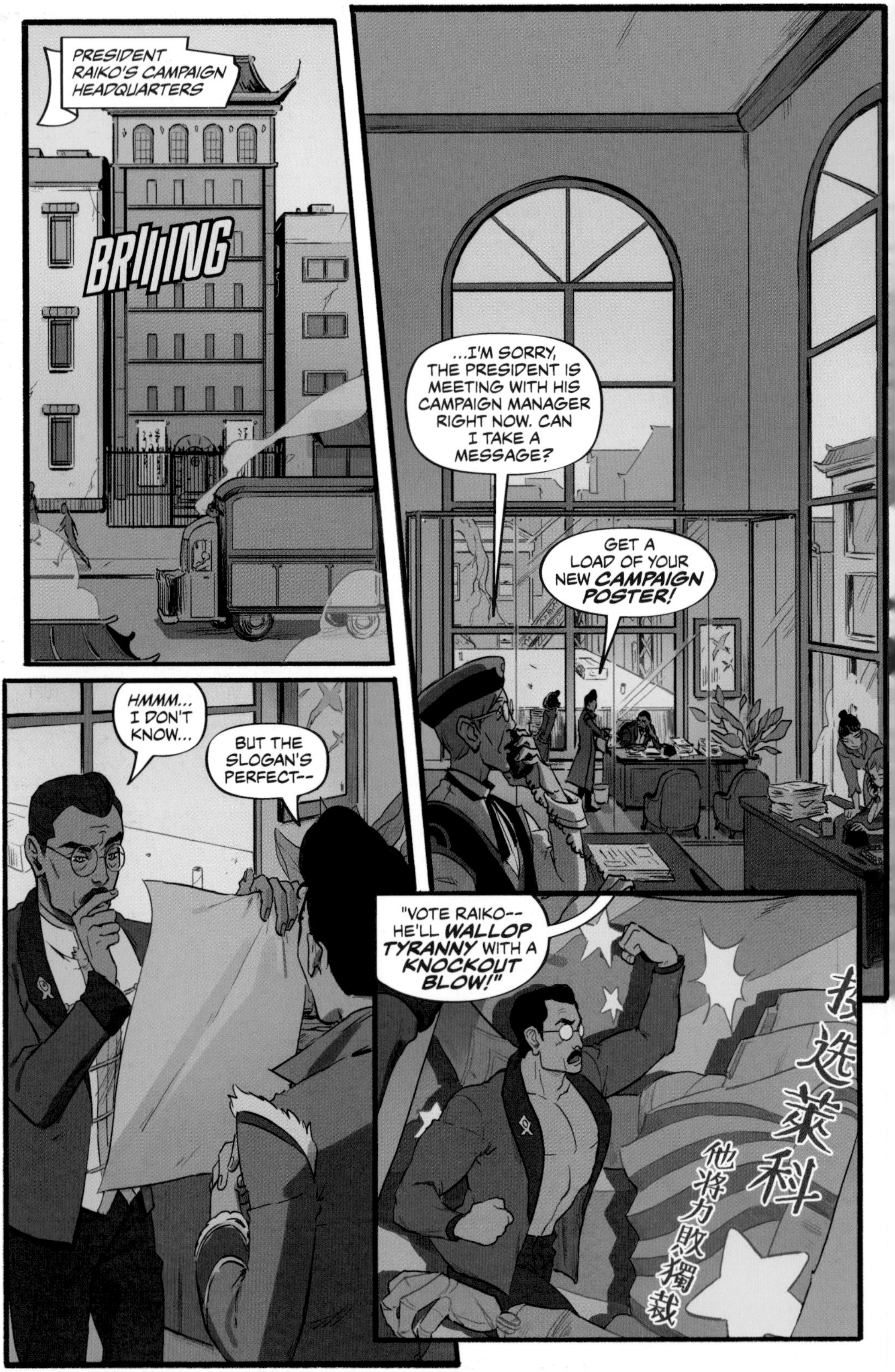
PRESIDENT RAIKO'S CAMPAIGN HEADQUARTERS
BRIIIING
...I'M SORRY, THE PRESIDENT IS MEETING WITH HIS CAMPAIGN MANAGER RIGHT NOW. CAN I TAKE A MESSAGE?
GET A LOAD OF YOUR NEW CAMPAIGN POSTER!
HMMM... I DON'T KNOW...
BUT THE SLOGAN'S PERFECT--
"VOTE RAIKO-- HE'LL WALLOP TYRANNY WITH A KNOCKOUT BLOW!"
投选莱科
他将力败獨裁

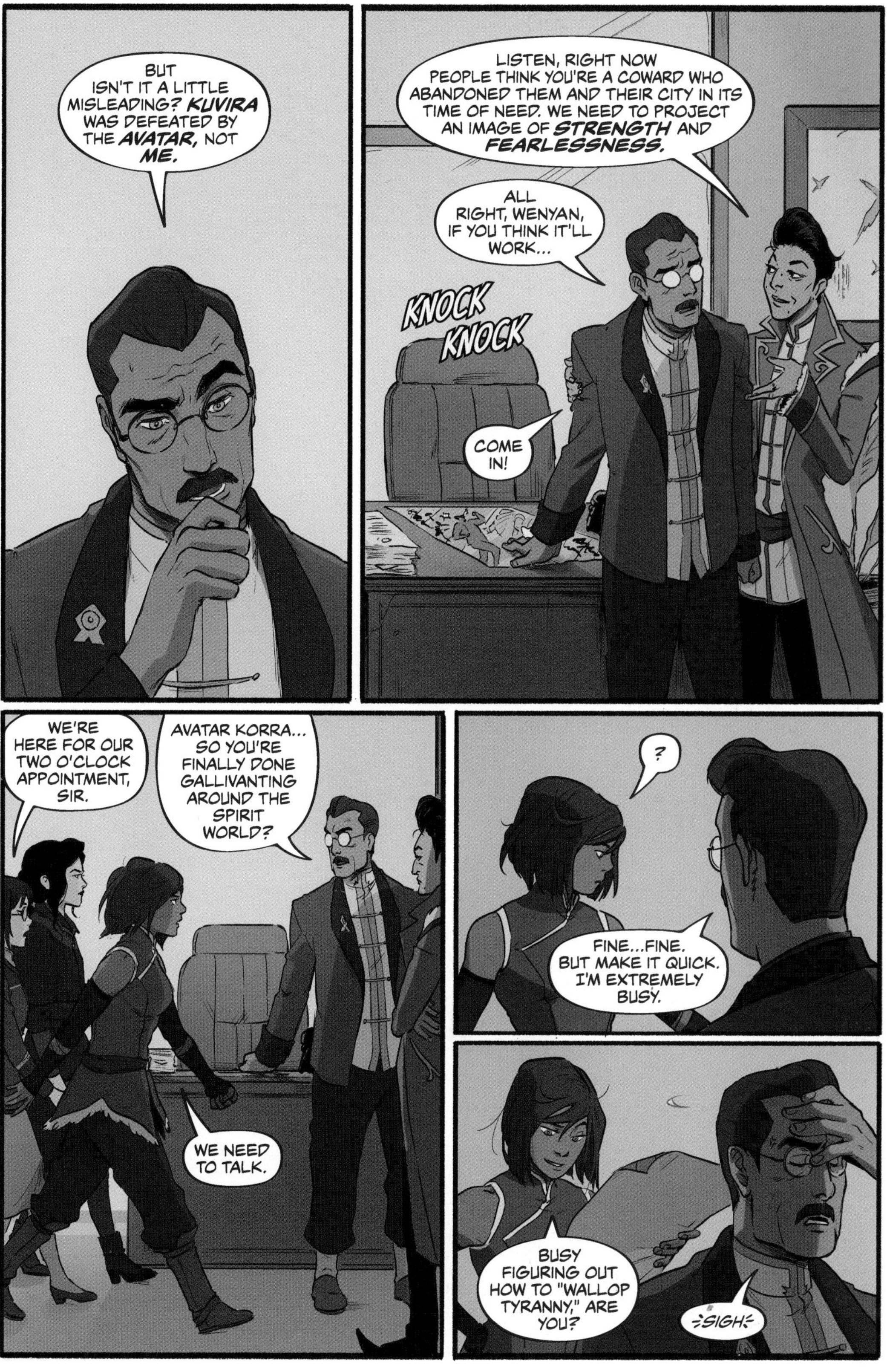
BUT ISN'T IT A LITTLE MISLEADING? KUVIRA WAS DEFEATED BY THE AVATAR, NOT ME.
LISTEN, RIGHT NOW PEOPLE THINK YOU'RE A COWARD WHO ABANDONED THEM AND THEIR CITY IN ITS TIME OF NEED. WE NEED TO PROJECT AN IMAGE OF STRENGTH AND FEARLESSNESS.
ALL RIGHT, WENYAN, IF YOU THINK IT'LL WORK...
KNOCK KNOCK
COME IN!
WE'RE HERE FOR OUR TWO O'CLOCK APPOINTMENT, SIR.
AVATAR KORRA... SO YOU'RE FINALLY DONE GALLIVANTING AROUND THE SPIRIT WORLD?
WE NEED TO TALK.
?
FINE...FINE. BUT MAKE IT QUICK. I'M EXTREMELY BUSY.
BUSY FIGURING OUT HOW TO "WALLOP TYRANNY," ARE YOU?
SIGH

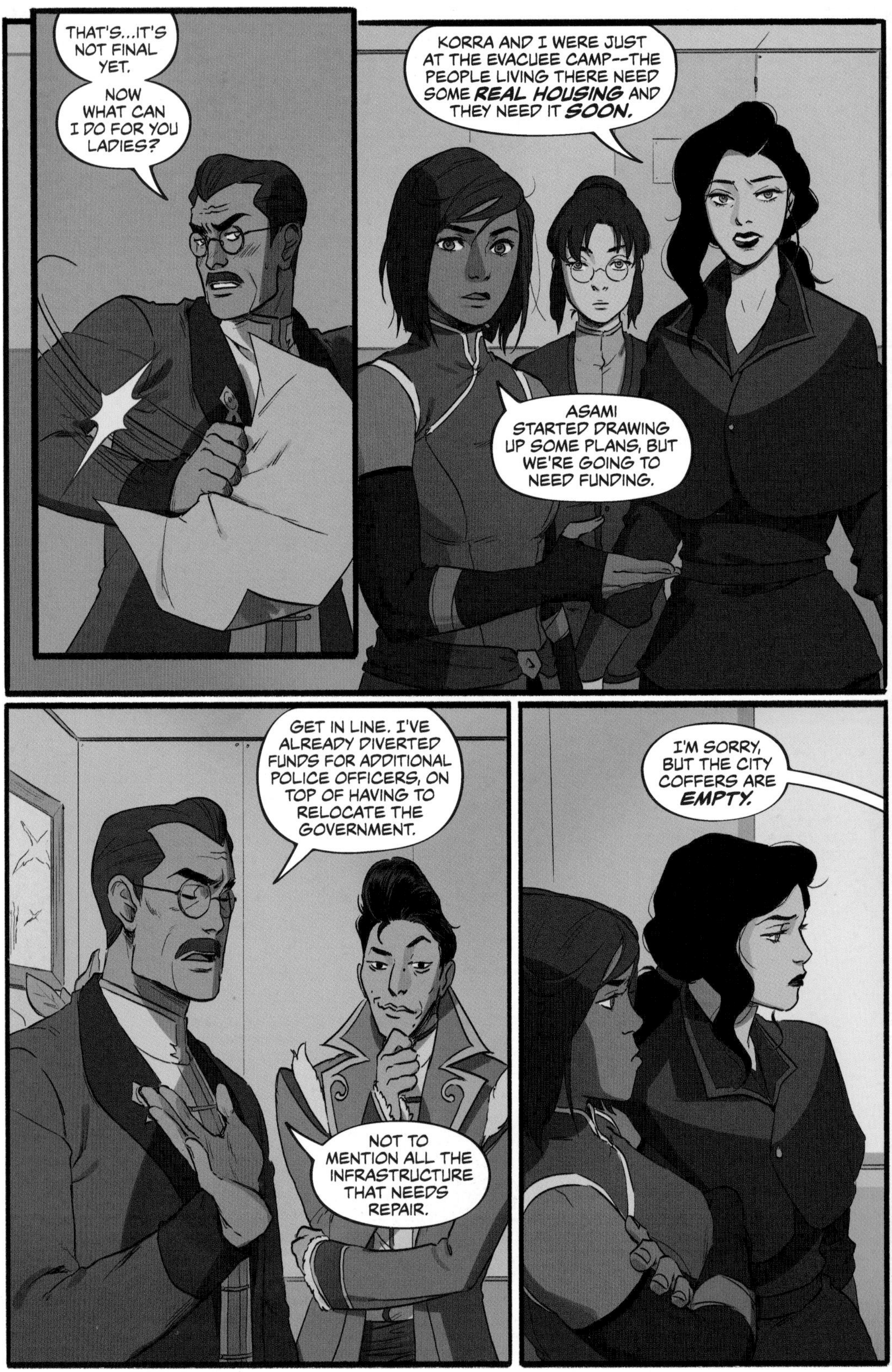
THAT'S...IT'S NOT FINAL YET.
NOW WHAT CAN I DO FOR YOU LADIES?
KORRA AND I WERE JUST AT THE EVACUEE CAMP--THE PEOPLE LIVING THERE NEED SOME REAL HOUSING AND THEY NEED IT SOON.
ASAMI STARTED DRAWING UP SOME PLANS, BUT WE'RE GOING TO NEED FUNDING.
GET IN LINE. I'VE ALREADY DIVERTED FUNDS FOR ADDITIONAL POLICE OFFICERS, ON TOP OF HAVING TO RELOCATE THE GOVERNMENT.
NOT TO MENTION ALL THE INFRASTRUCTURE THAT NEEDS REPAIR.
I'M SORRY, BUT THE CITY COFFERS ARE EMPTY.

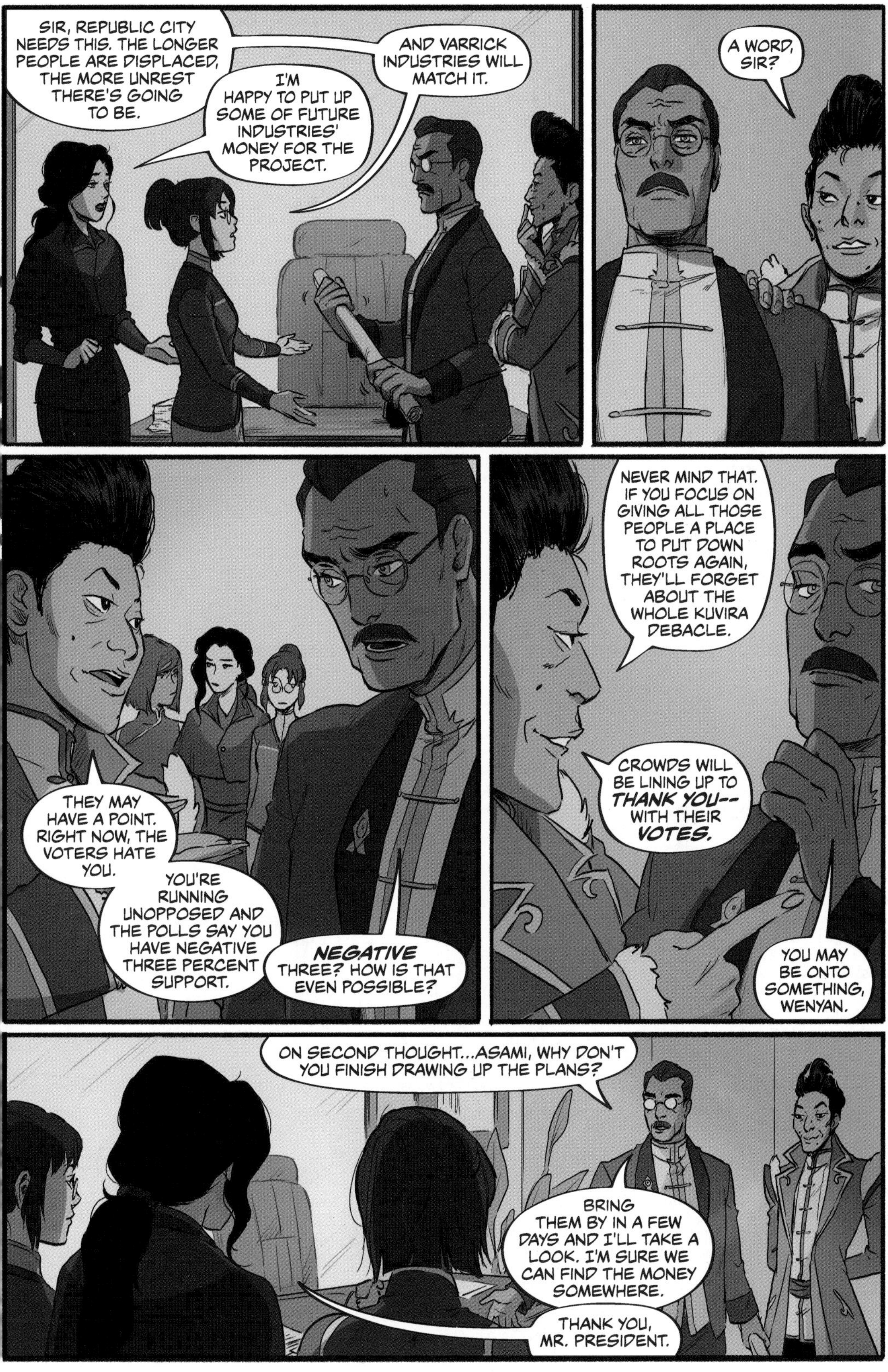
SIR, REPUBLIC CITY NEEDS THIS. THE LONGER PEOPLE ARE DISPLACED, THE MORE UNREST THERE'S GOING TO BE.
I'M HAPPY TO PUT UP SOME OF FUTURE INDUSTRIES' MONEY FOR THE PROJECT.
AND VARRICK INDUSTRIES WILL MATCH IT.
A WORD, SIR?
THEY MAY HAVE A POINT. RIGHT NOW, THE VOTERS HATE YOU.
YOU'RE RUNNING UNOPPOSED AND THE POLLS SAY YOU HAVE NEGATIVE THREE PERCENT SUPPORT.
NEGATIVE THREE? HOW IS THAT EVEN POSSIBLE?
NEVER MIND THAT. IF YOU FOCUS ON GIVING ALL THOSE PEOPLE A PLACE TO PUT DOWN ROOTS AGAIN, THEY'LL FORGET ABOUT THE WHOLE KUVIRA DEBACLE.
CROWDS WILL BE LINING UP TO *THANK YOU*-- WITH THEIR *VOTES.*
YOU MAY BE ONTO SOMETHING, WENYAN.
ON SECOND THOUGHT...ASAMI, WHY DON'T YOU FINISH DRAWING UP THE PLANS?
BRING THEM BY IN A FEW DAYS AND I'LL TAKE A LOOK. I'M SURE WE CAN FIND THE MONEY SOMEWHERE.
THANK YOU, MR. PRESIDENT.

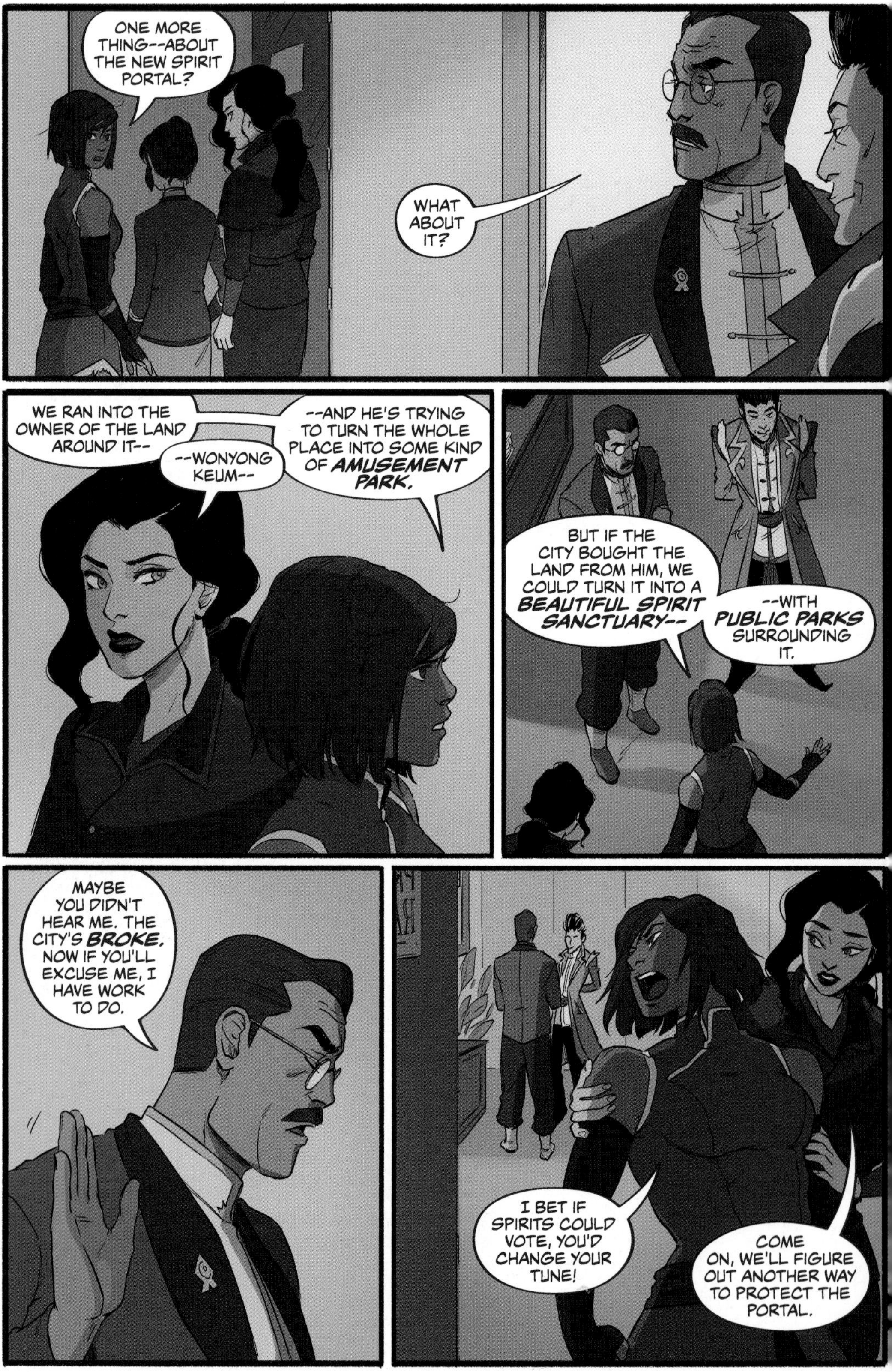
ONE MORE THING--ABOUT THE NEW SPIRIT PORTAL?
WHAT ABOUT IT?
WE RAN INTO THE OWNER OF THE LAND AROUND IT--
--WONYONG KEUM--
--AND HE'S TRYING TO TURN THE WHOLE PLACE INTO SOME KIND OF AMUSEMENT PARK.
BUT IF THE CITY BOUGHT THE LAND FROM HIM, WE COULD TURN IT INTO A BEAUTIFUL SPIRIT SANCTUARY--
--WITH PUBLIC PARKS SURROUNDING IT.
MAYBE YOU DIDN'T HEAR ME. THE CITY'S BROKE. NOW IF YOU'LL EXCUSE ME, I HAVE WORK TO DO.
I BET IF SPIRITS COULD VOTE, YOU'D CHANGE YOUR TUNE!
COME ON, WE'LL FIGURE OUT ANOTHER WAY TO PROTECT THE PORTAL.

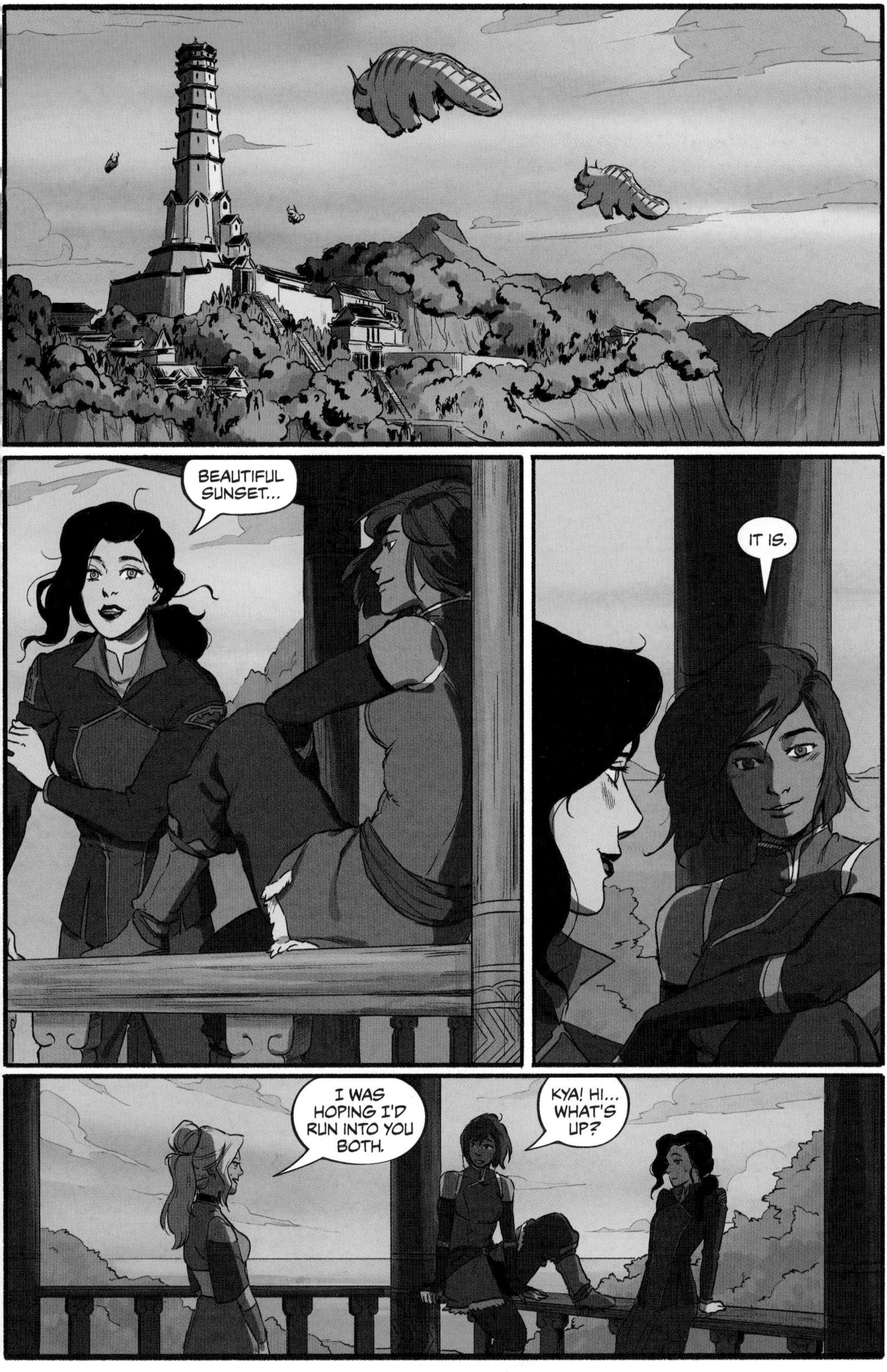
BEAUTIFUL SUNSET...
IT IS.
I WAS HOPING I'D RUN INTO YOU BOTH.
KYA! HI... WHAT'S UP?

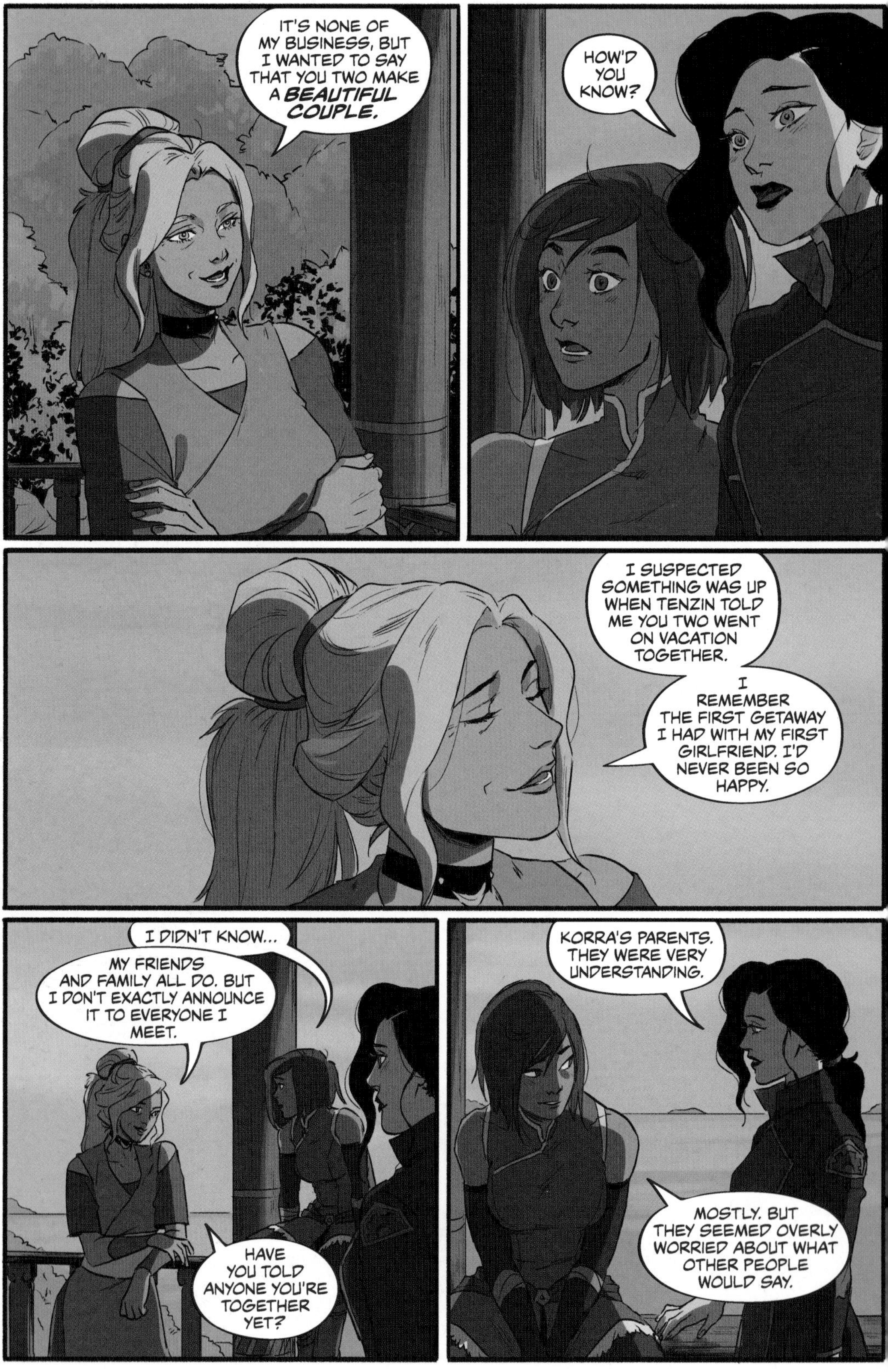
IT'S NONE OF MY BUSINESS, BUT I WANTED TO SAY THAT YOU TWO MAKE A *BEAUTIFUL COUPLE.*
HOW'D YOU KNOW?
I SUSPECTED SOMETHING WAS UP WHEN TENZIN TOLD ME YOU TWO WENT ON VACATION TOGETHER.
I REMEMBER THE FIRST GETAWAY I HAD WITH MY FIRST GIRLFRIEND. I'D NEVER BEEN SO HAPPY.
I DIDN'T KNOW...
MY FRIENDS AND FAMILY ALL DO. BUT I DON'T EXACTLY ANNOUNCE IT TO EVERYONE I MEET.
HAVE YOU TOLD ANYONE YOU'RE TOGETHER YET?
KORRA'S PARENTS. THEY WERE VERY UNDERSTANDING.
MOSTLY. BUT THEY SEEMED OVERLY WORRIED ABOUT WHAT OTHER PEOPLE WOULD SAY.

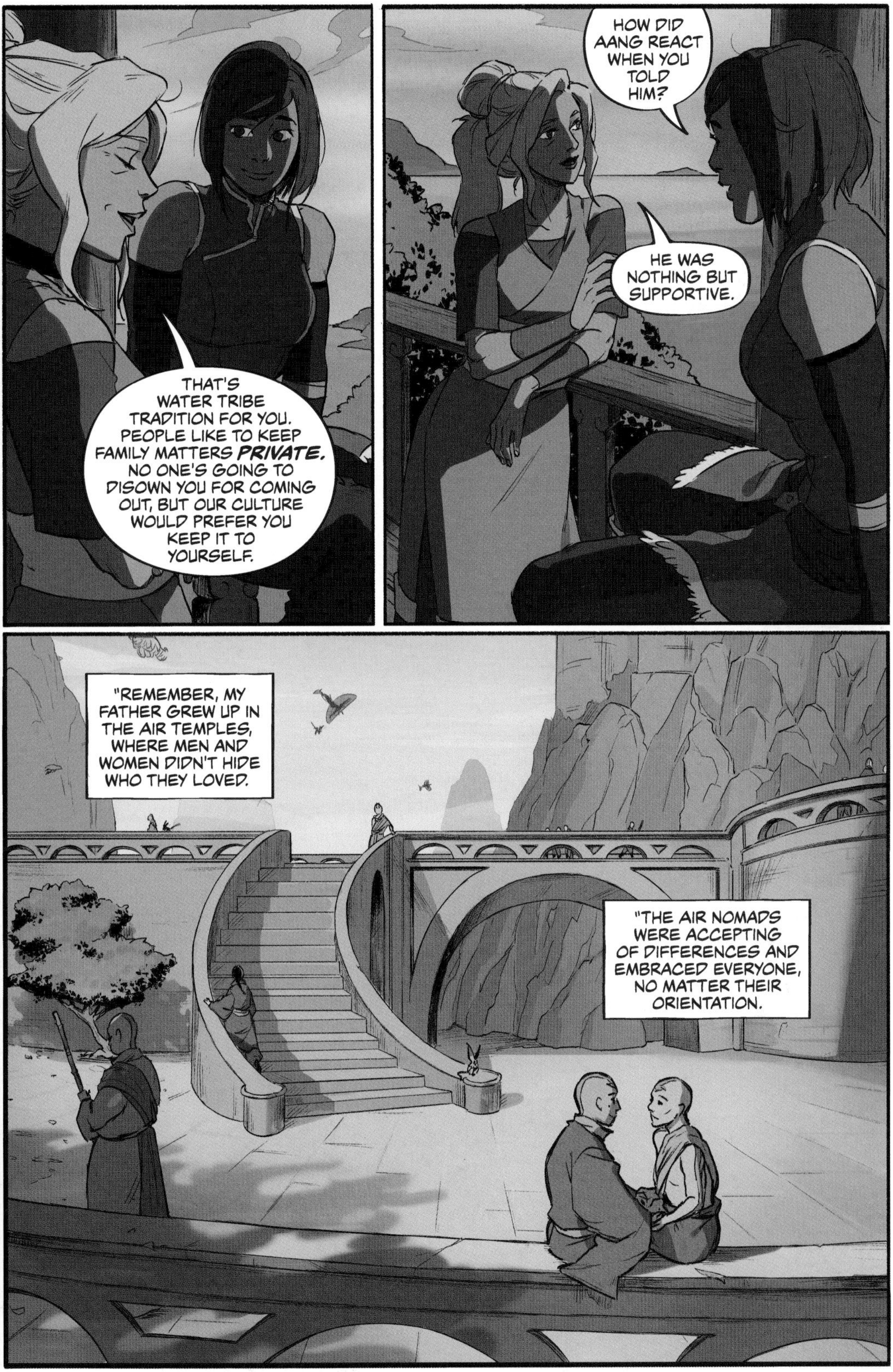
THAT'S WATER TRIBE TRADITION FOR YOU. PEOPLE LIKE TO KEEP FAMILY MATTERS PRIVATE. NO ONE'S GOING TO DISOWN YOU FOR COMING OUT, BUT OUR CULTURE WOULD PREFER YOU KEEP IT TO YOURSELF.
HOW DID AANG REACT WHEN YOU TOLD HIM?
HE WAS NOTHING BUT SUPPORTIVE.
"REMEMBER, MY FATHER GREW UP IN THE AIR TEMPLES, WHERE MEN AND WOMEN DIDN'T HIDE WHO THEY LOVED.
"THE AIR NOMADS WERE ACCEPTING OF DIFFERENCES AND EMBRACED EVERYONE, NO MATTER THEIR ORIENTATION.

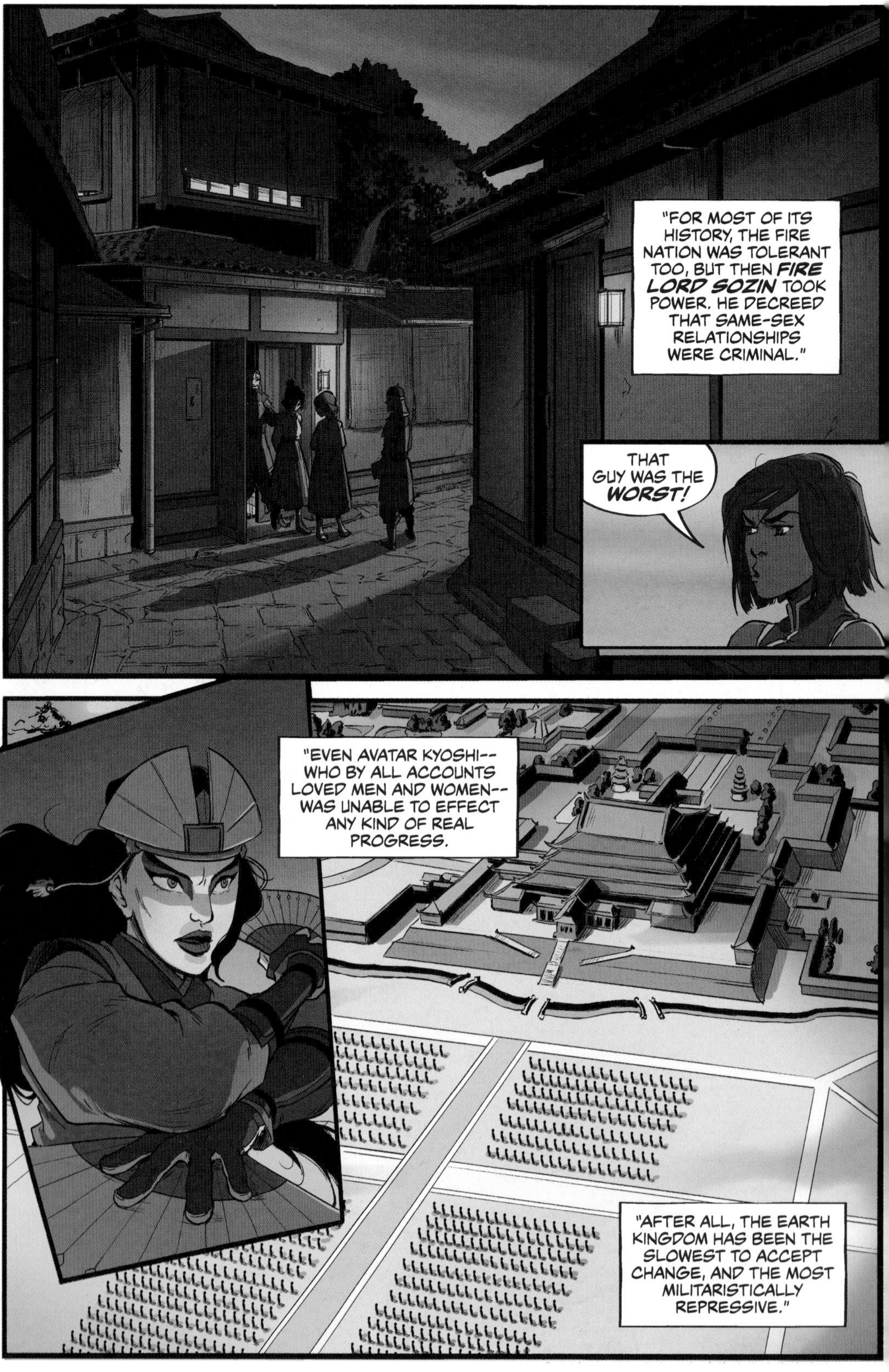
"FOR MOST OF ITS HISTORY, THE FIRE NATION WAS TOLERANT TOO, BUT THEN FIRE LORD SOZIN TOOK POWER. HE DECREED THAT SAME-SEX RELATIONSHIPS WERE CRIMINAL."
THAT GUY WAS THE WORST!
"EVEN AVATAR KYOSHI-- WHO BY ALL ACCOUNTS LOVED MEN AND WOMEN-- WAS UNABLE TO EFFECT ANY KIND OF REAL PROGRESS.
"AFTER ALL, THE EARTH KINGDOM HAS BEEN THE SLOWEST TO ACCEPT CHANGE, AND THE MOST MILITARISTICALLY REPRESSIVE."

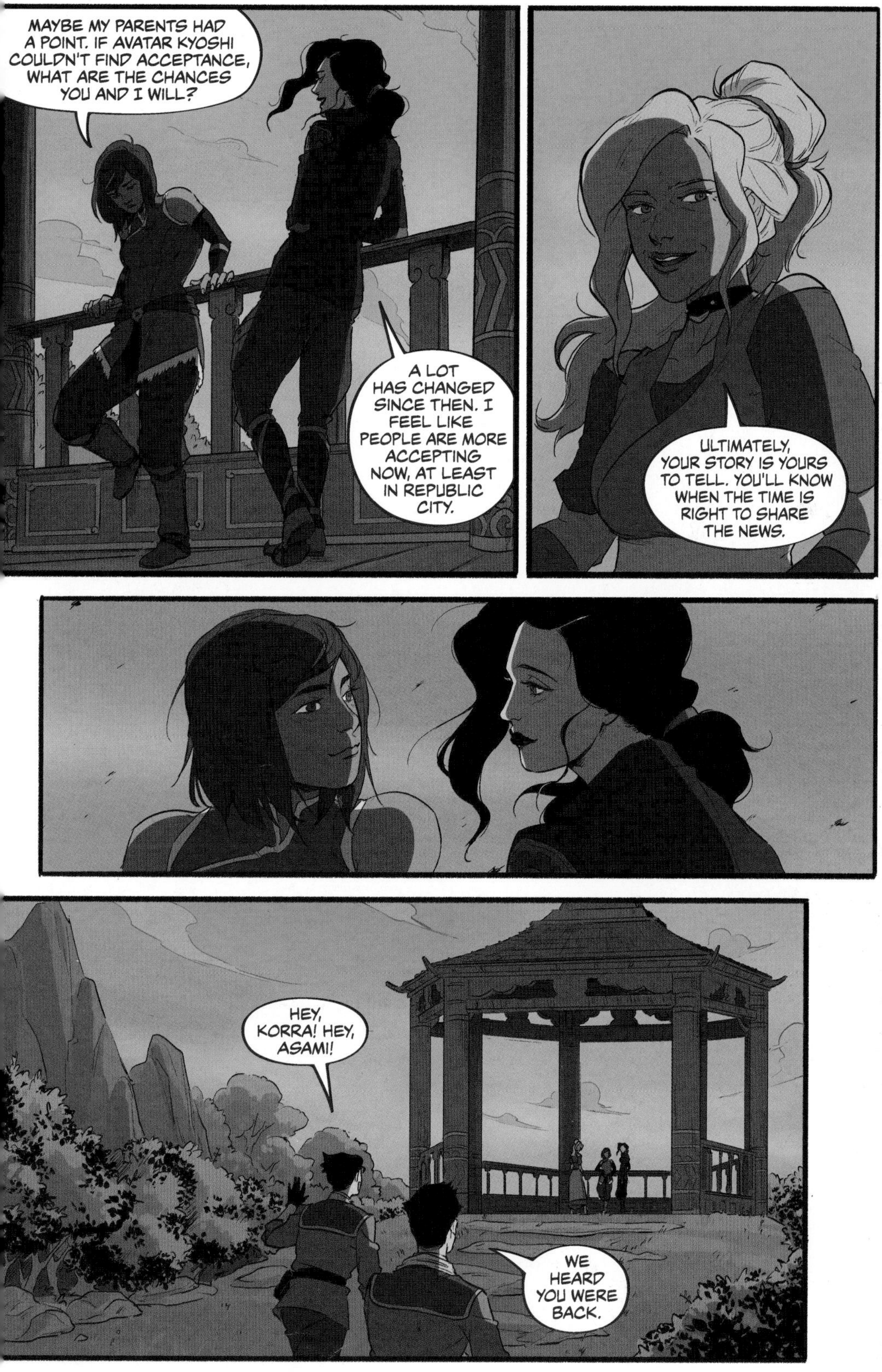
MAYBE MY PARENTS HAD A POINT. IF AVATAR KYOSHI COULDN'T FIND ACCEPTANCE, WHAT ARE THE CHANCES YOU AND I WILL?
A LOT HAS CHANGED SINCE THEN. I FEEL LIKE PEOPLE ARE MORE ACCEPTING NOW, AT LEAST IN REPUBLIC CITY.
ULTIMATELY, YOUR STORY IS YOURS TO TELL. YOU'LL KNOW WHEN THE TIME IS RIGHT TO SHARE THE NEWS.
HEY, KORRA! HEY, ASAMI!
WE HEARD YOU WERE BACK.

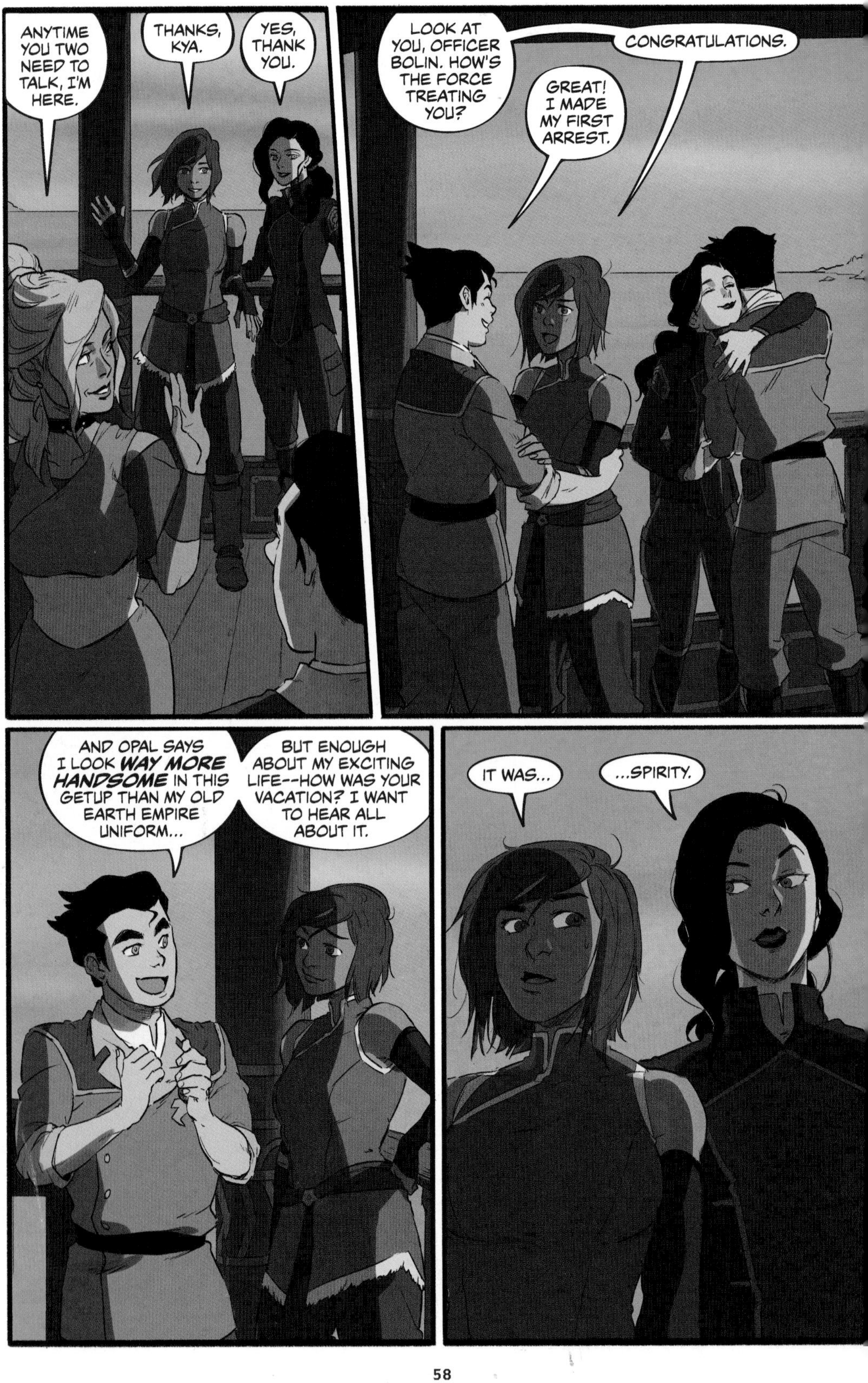
ANYTIME YOU TWO NEED TO TALK, I'M HERE.
THANKS, KYA.
YES, THANK YOU.
LOOK AT YOU, OFFICER BOLIN. HOW'S THE FORCE TREATING YOU?
CONGRATULATIONS.
GREAT! I MADE MY FIRST ARREST.
AND OPAL SAYS I LOOK **WAY MORE HANDSOME** IN THIS GETUP THAN MY OLD EARTH EMPIRE UNIFORM...
BUT ENOUGH ABOUT MY EXCITING LIFE--HOW WAS YOUR VACATION? I WANT TO HEAR ALL ABOUT IT.
IT WAS...
...SPIRITY.

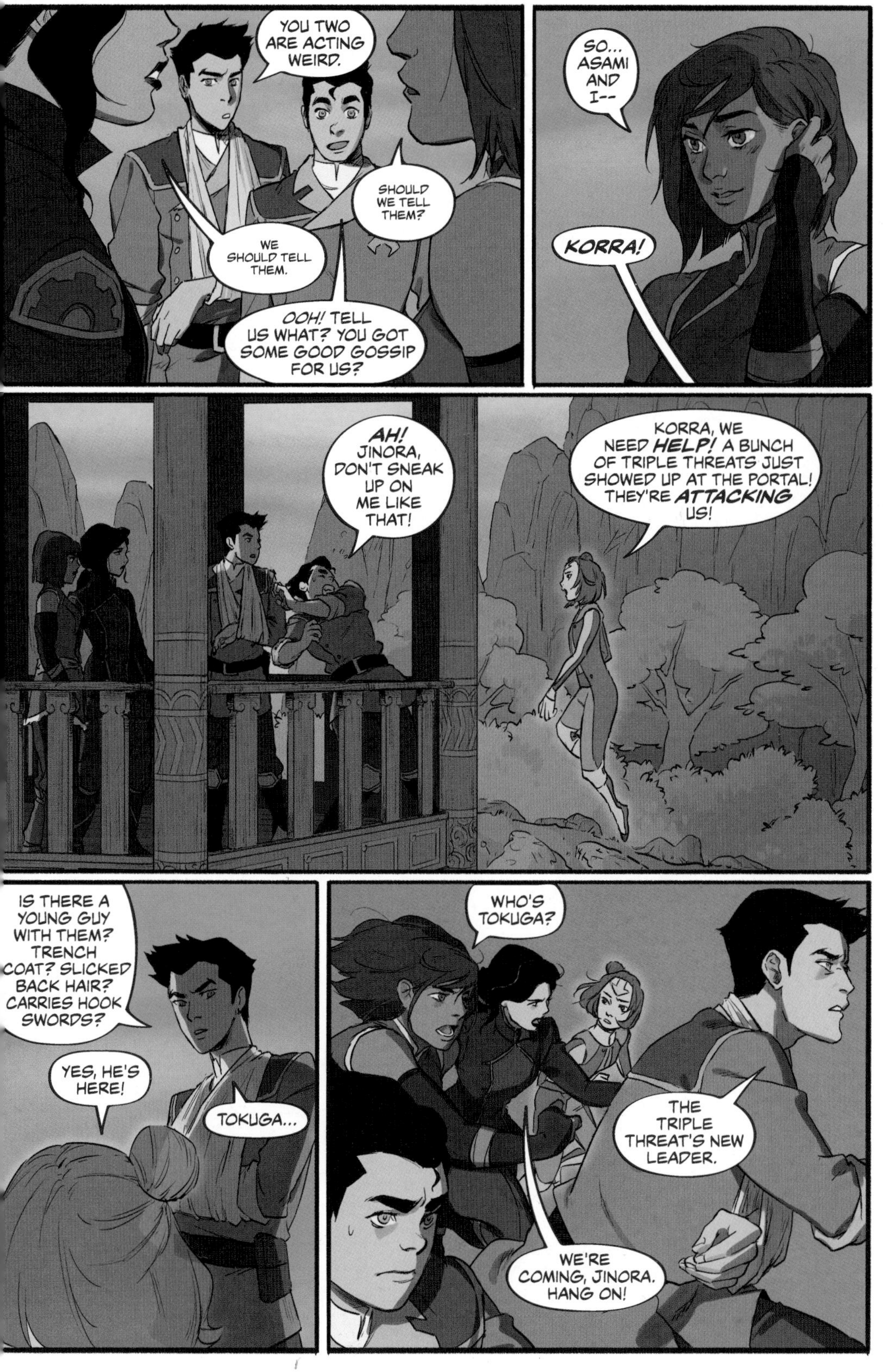

YOU TWO ARE ACTING WEIRD.
WE SHOULD TELL THEM.
SHOULD WE TELL THEM?
OOH! TELL US WHAT? YOU GOT SOME GOOD GOSSIP FOR US?
SO... ASAMI AND I--
KORRA!
AH! JINORA, DON'T SNEAK UP ON ME LIKE THAT!
KORRA, WE NEED HELP! A BUNCH OF TRIPLE THREATS JUST SHOWED UP AT THE PORTAL! THEY'RE ATTACKING US!
IS THERE A YOUNG GUY WITH THEM? TRENCH COAT? SLICKED BACK HAIR? CARRIES HOOK SWORDS?
YES, HE'S HERE!
TOKUGA...
WHO'S TOKUGA?
THE TRIPLE THREAT'S NEW LEADER.
WE'RE COMING, JINORA. HANG ON!

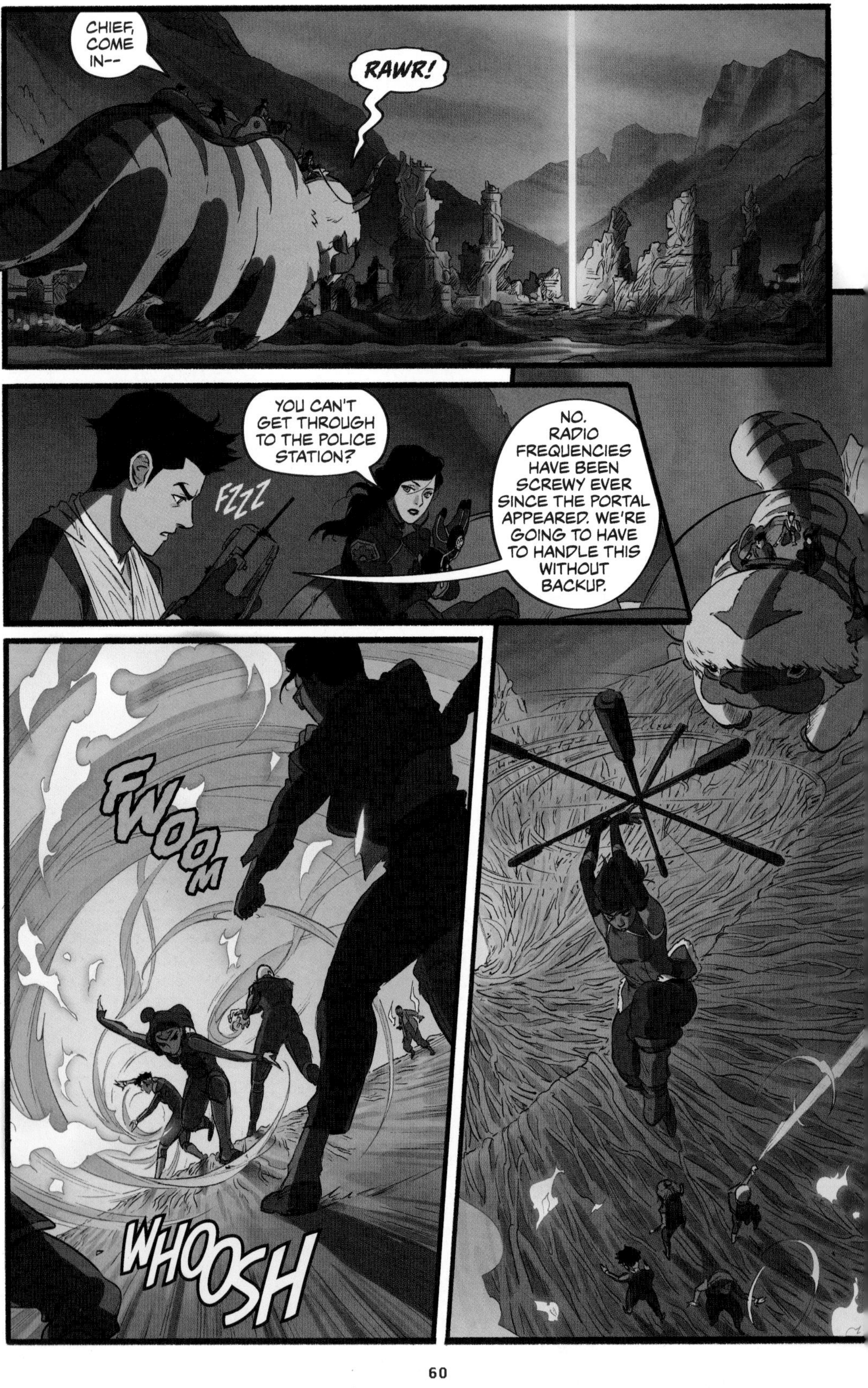
CHIEF, COME IN--
RAWR!
YOU CAN'T GET THROUGH TO THE POLICE STATION?
FZZZ
NO. RADIO FREQUENCIES HAVE BEEN SCREWY EVER SINCE THE PORTAL APPEARED. WE'RE GOING TO HAVE TO HANDLE THIS WITHOUT BACKUP.
FWOOM
WHOOSH

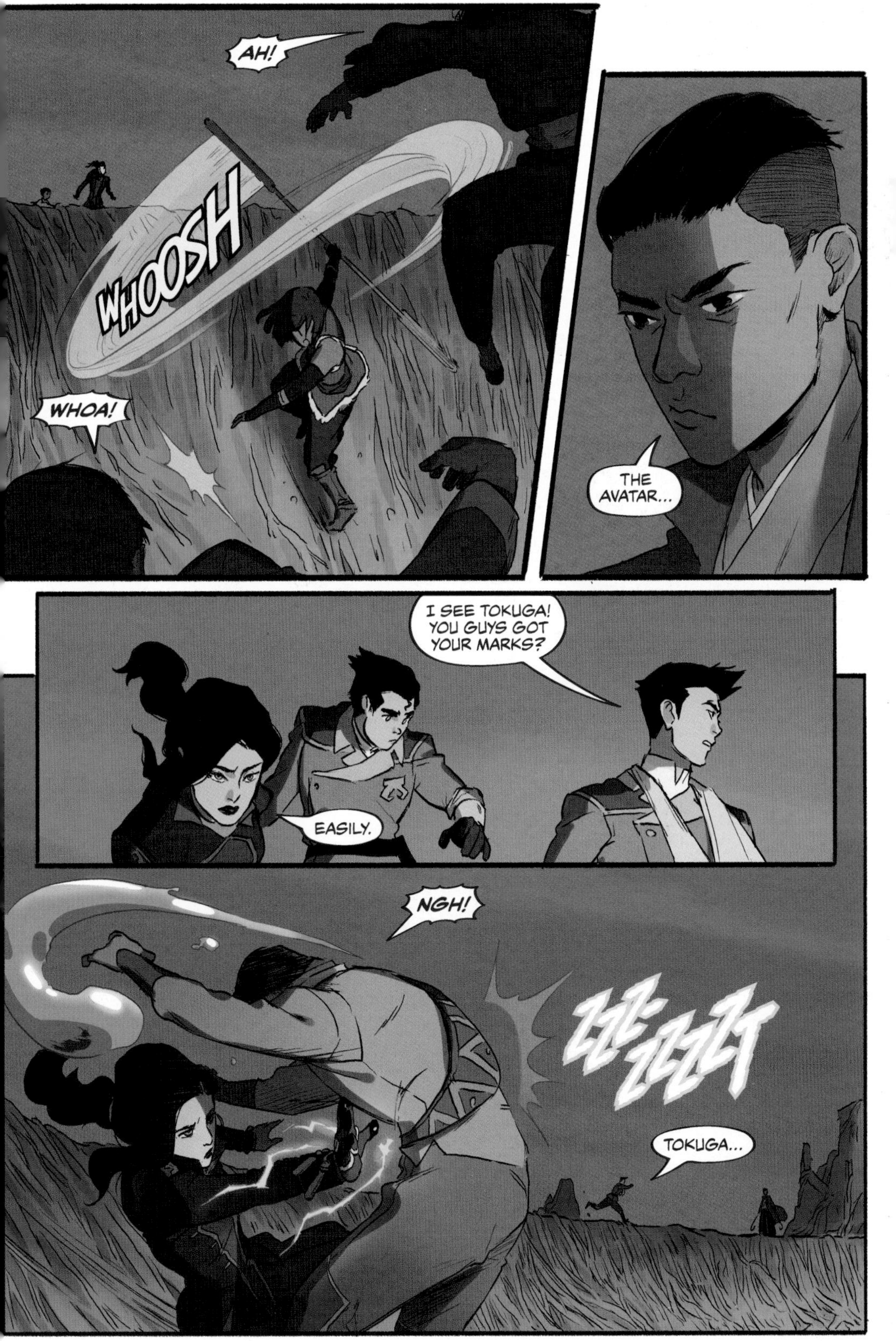
AH!
WHOOSH
WHOA!
THE AVATAR...
I SEE TOKUGA! YOU GUYS GOT YOUR MARKS?
EASILY.
NGH!
ZZZ-ZZZZZT
TOKUGA...

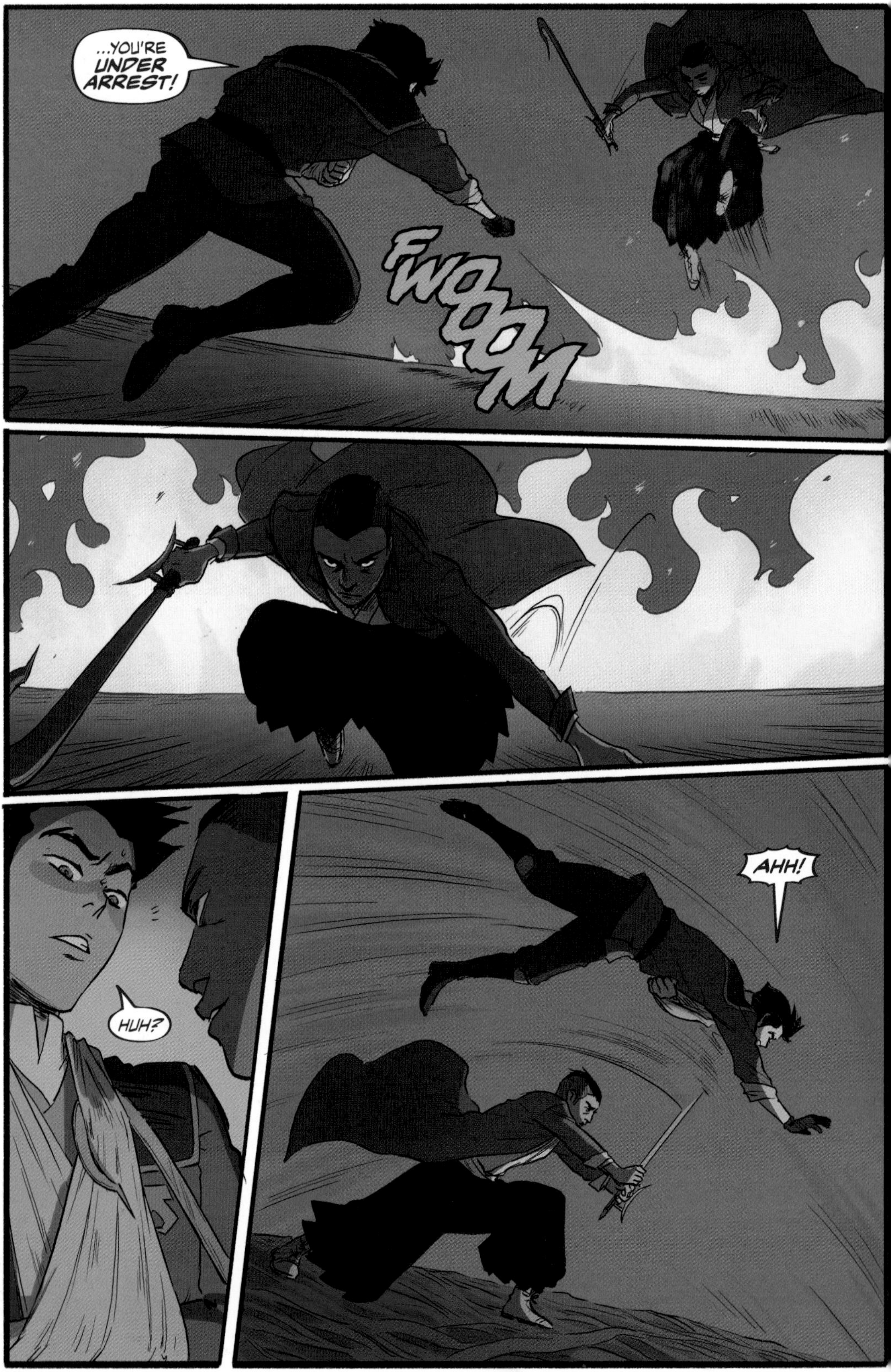
...YOU'RE UNDER ARREST!
FWOOOM
HUH?
AHH!

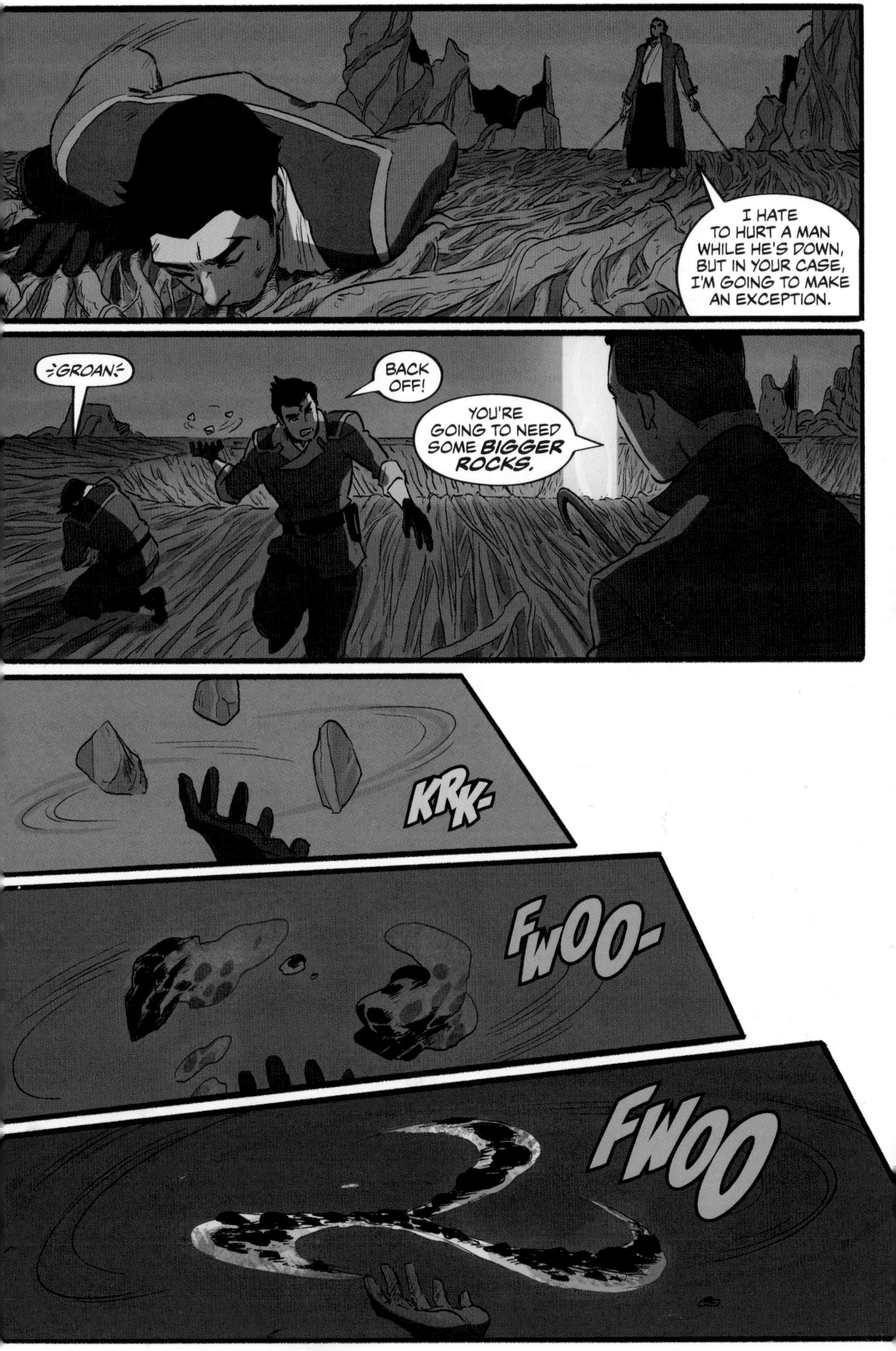
I HATE TO HURT A MAN WHILE HE'S DOWN, BUT IN YOUR CASE, I'M GOING TO MAKE AN EXCEPTION.
GROAN
BACK OFF!
YOU'RE GOING TO NEED SOME **BIGGER ROCKS.**
KRK-
FWOO-
FWOO

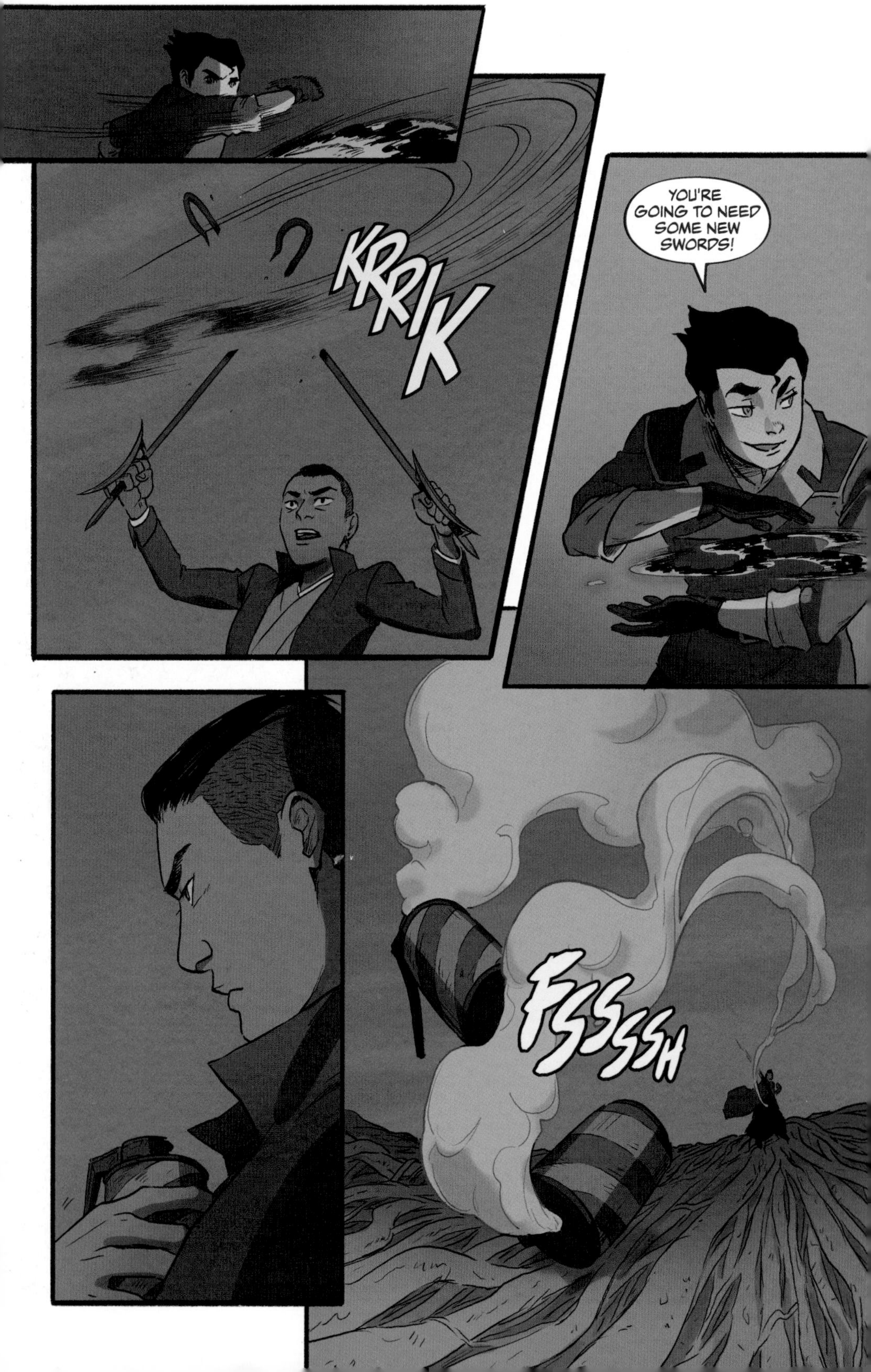
KRRIK
YOU'RE GOING TO NEED SOME NEW SWORDS!
FSSSSH

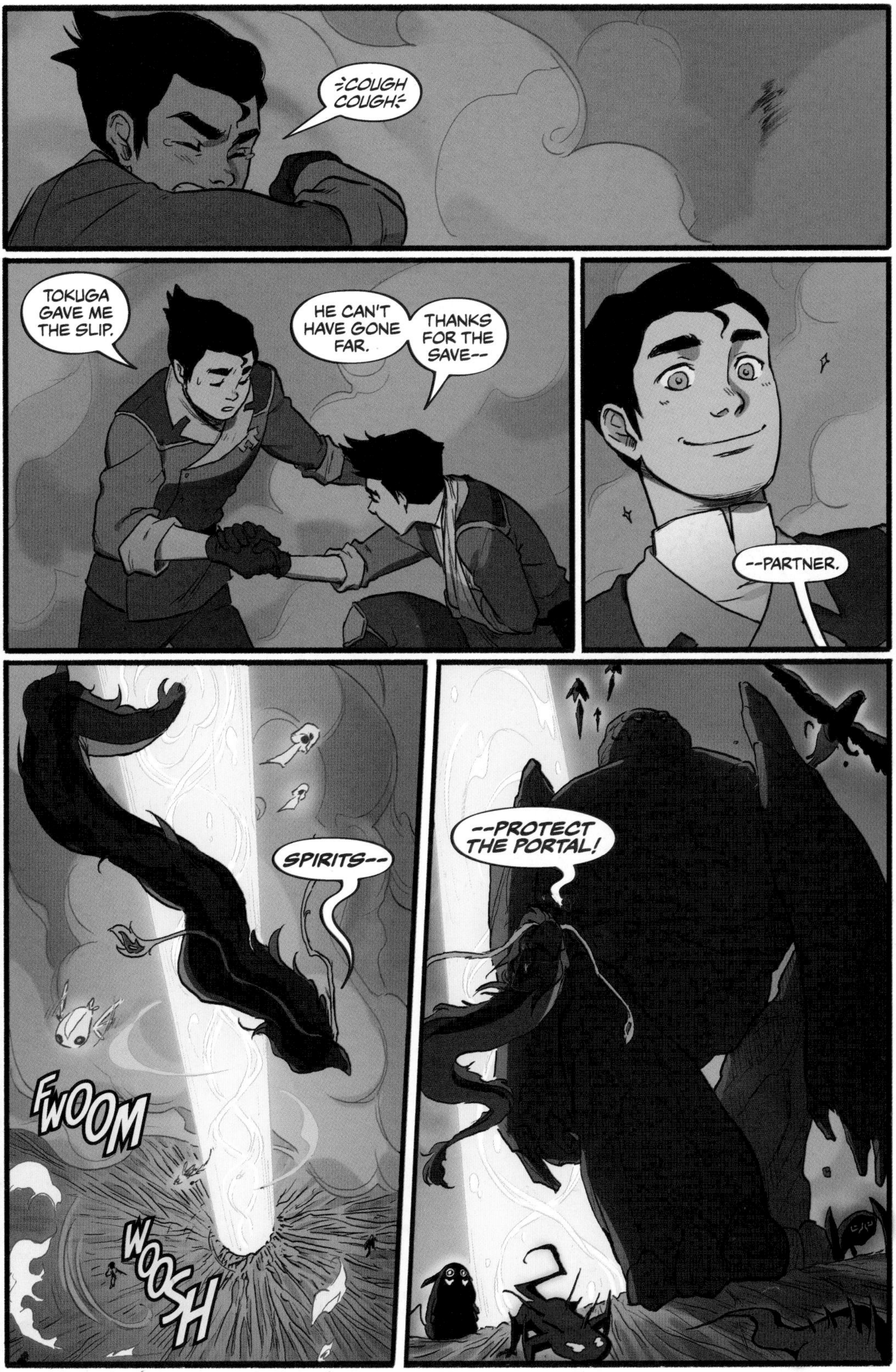

COUGH COUGH
TOKUGA GAVE ME THE SLIP.
HE CAN'T HAVE GONE FAR.
THANKS FOR THE SAVE--
--PARTNER.
FWOOM
WOOSH
SPIRITS--
--PROTECT THE PORTAL!

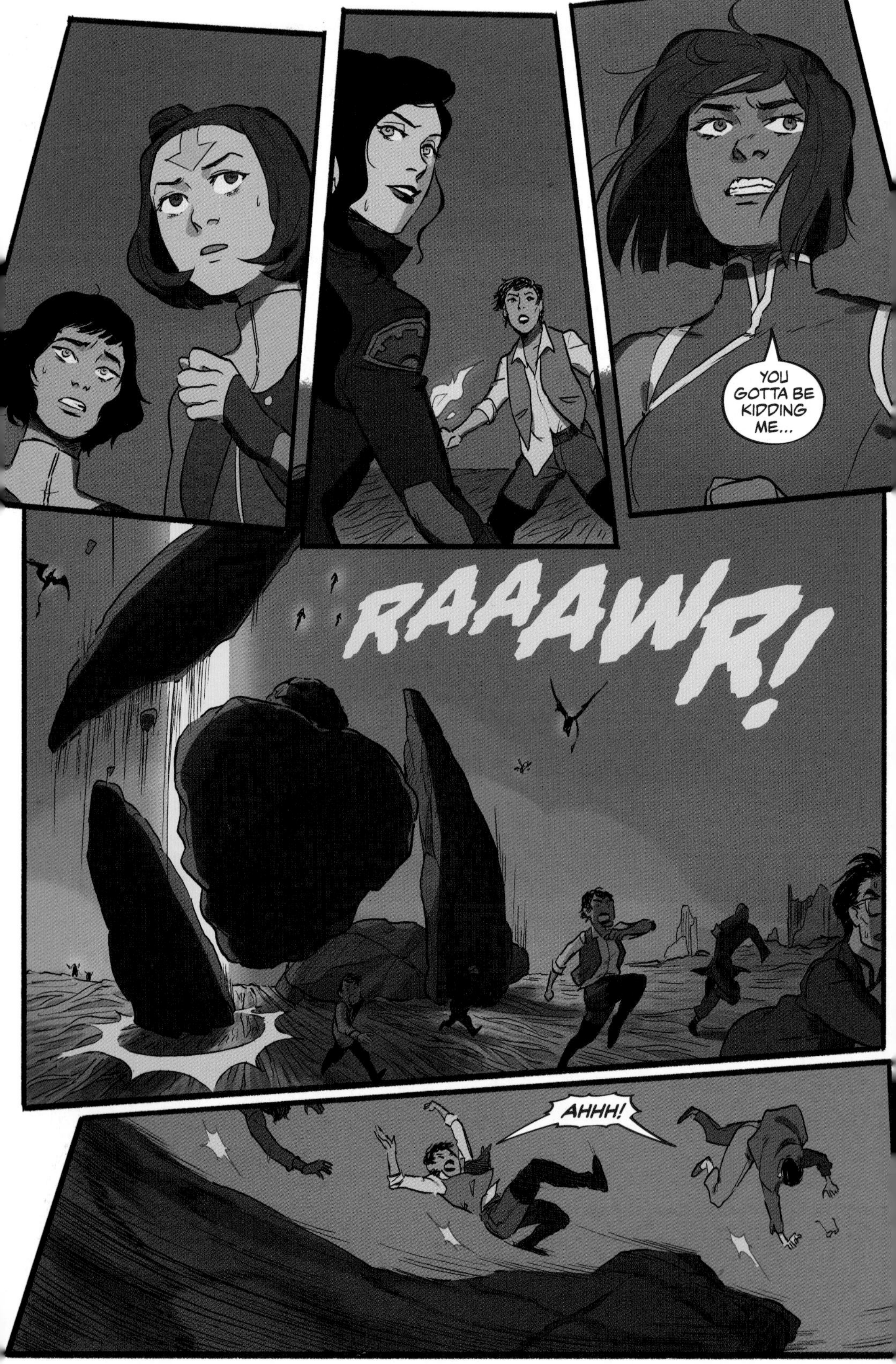
YOU GOTTA BE KIDDING ME...
RAAAWR!
AHHH!

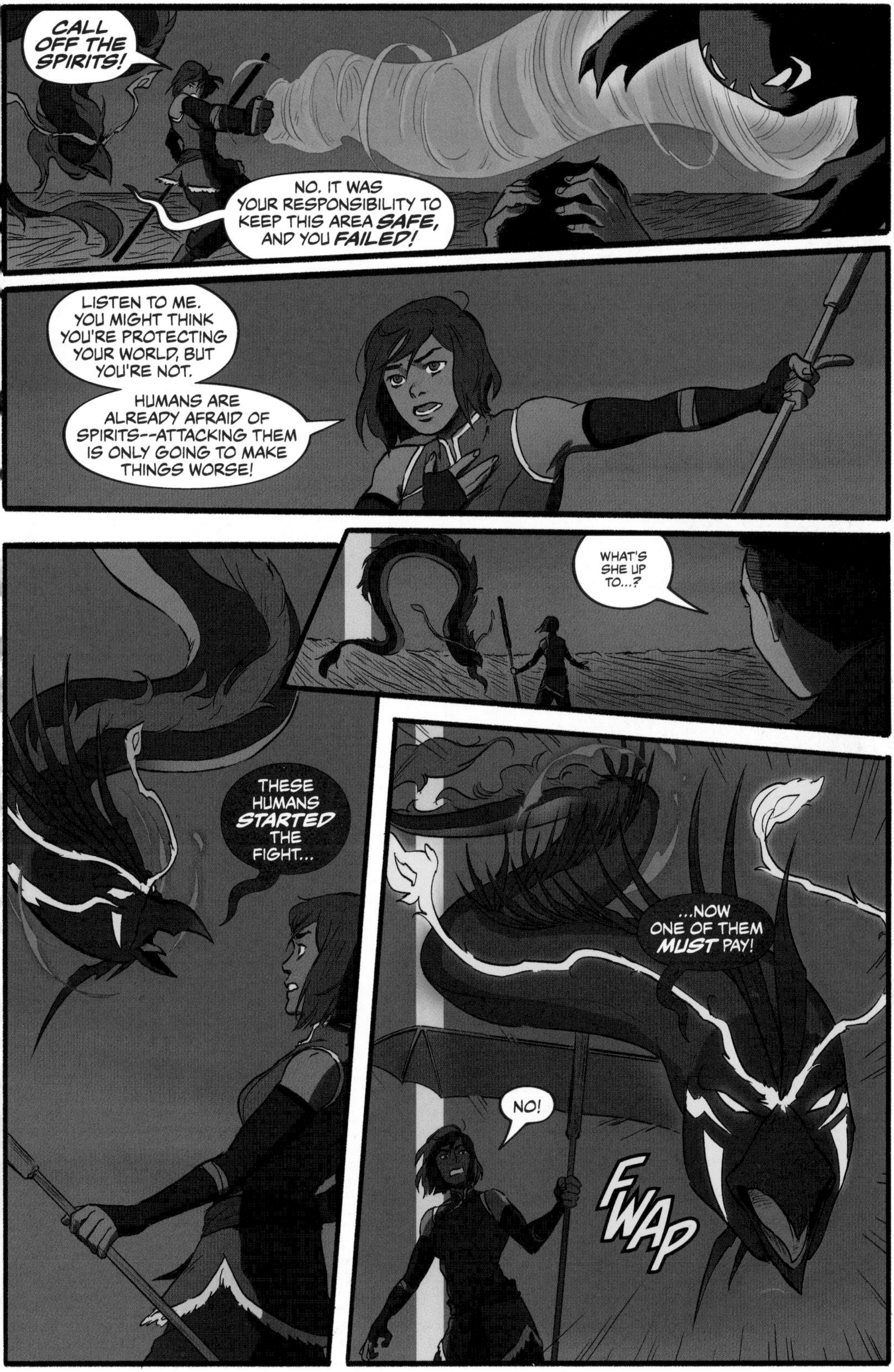
CALL OFF THE SPIRITS!
NO. IT WAS YOUR RESPONSIBILITY TO KEEP THIS AREA SAFE, AND YOU FAILED!
LISTEN TO ME. YOU MIGHT THINK YOU'RE PROTECTING YOUR WORLD, BUT YOU'RE NOT.
HUMANS ARE ALREADY AFRAID OF SPIRITS--ATTACKING THEM IS ONLY GOING TO MAKE THINGS WORSE!
WHAT'S SHE UP TO...?
THESE HUMANS STARTED THE FIGHT...
...NOW ONE OF THEM MUST PAY!
NO!
FWAP

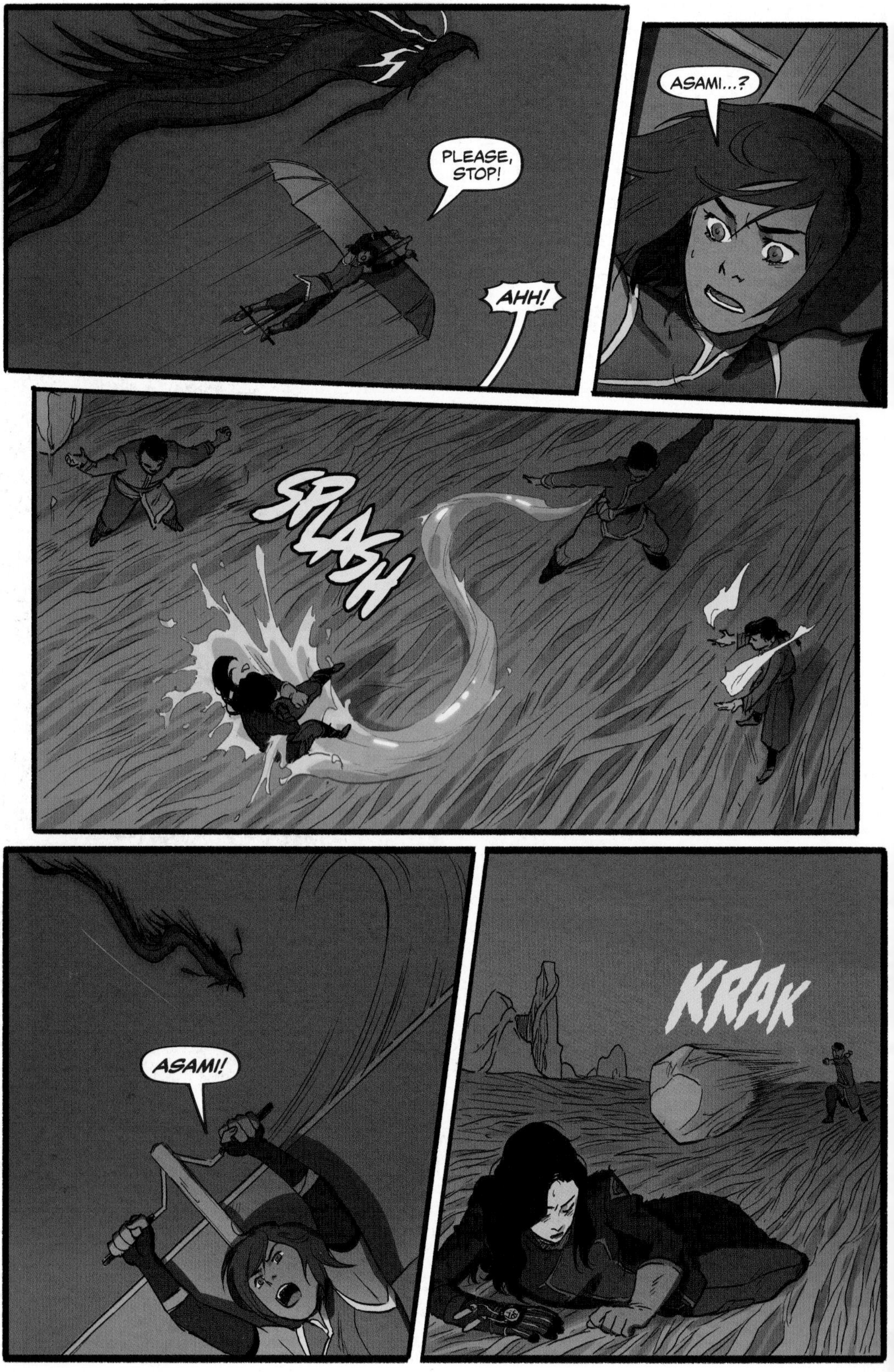
PLEASE, STOP!
AHH!
ASAMI...?
SPLASH
ASAMI!
KRAK

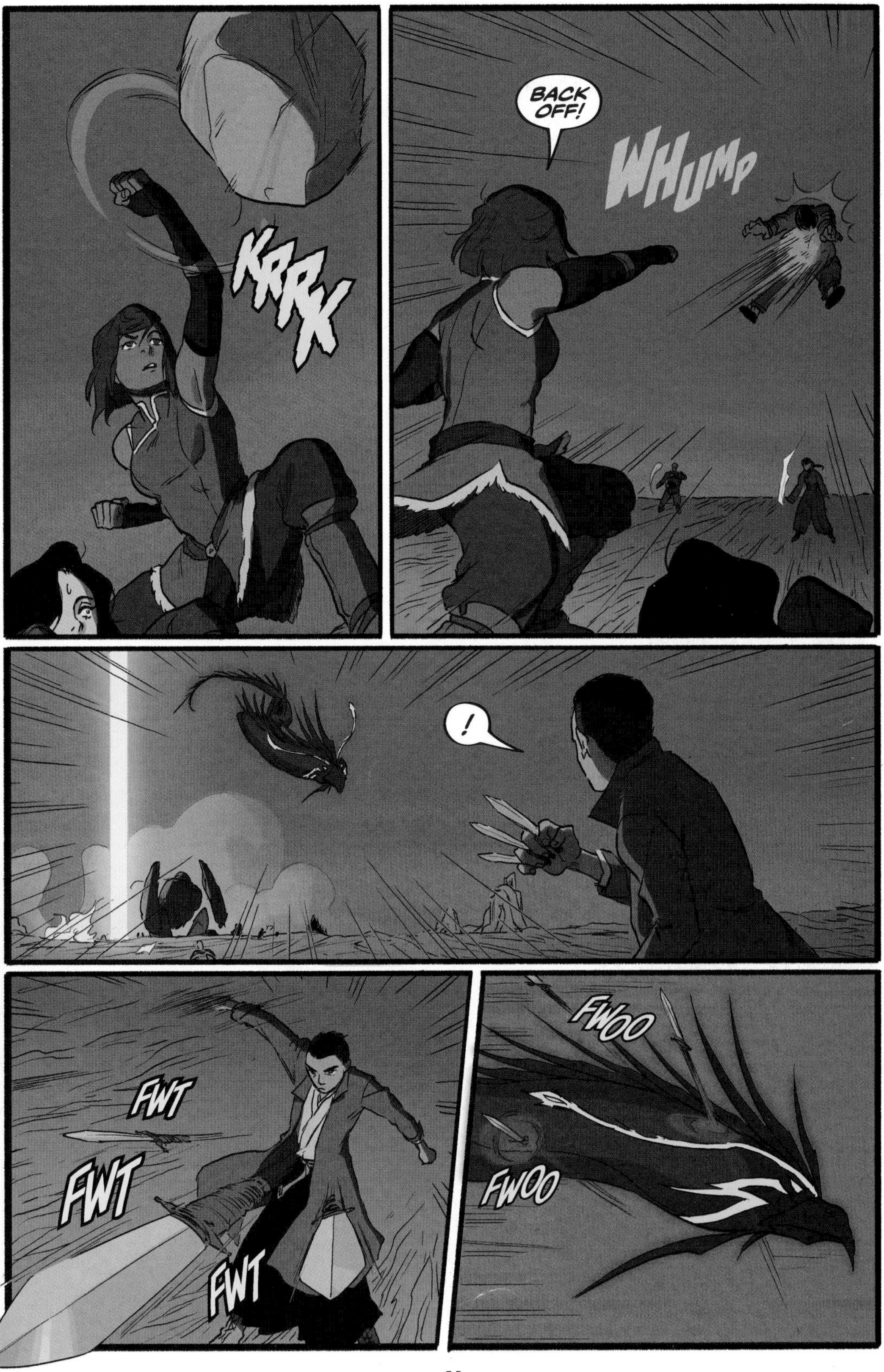
KRRK
BACK OFF!
WHUMP
!
FWT
FWT
FWT
FWOO
FWOO

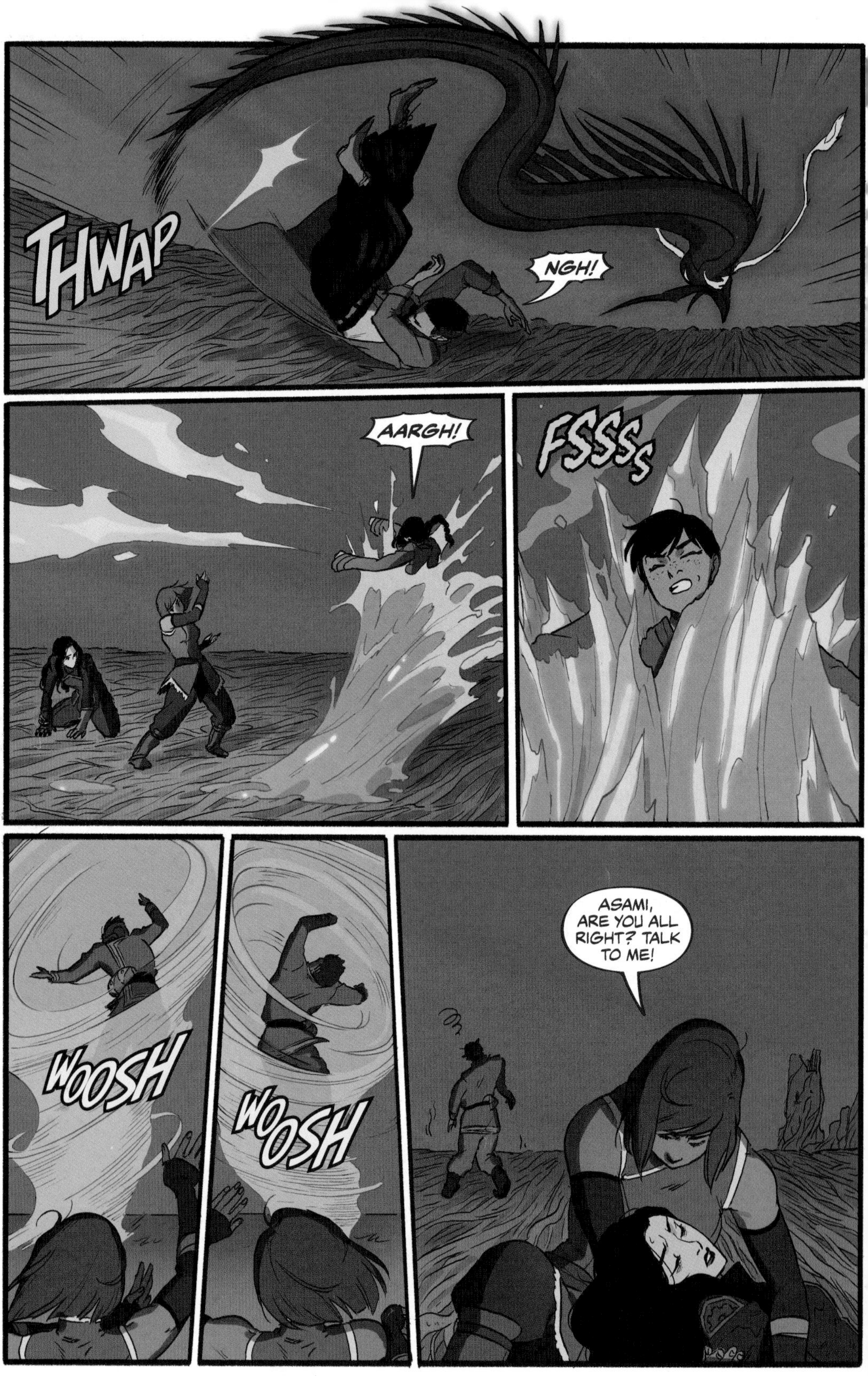
THWAP
NGH!
AARGH!
FSSSS
WOOSH
WOOSH
ASAMI, ARE YOU ALL RIGHT? TALK TO ME!

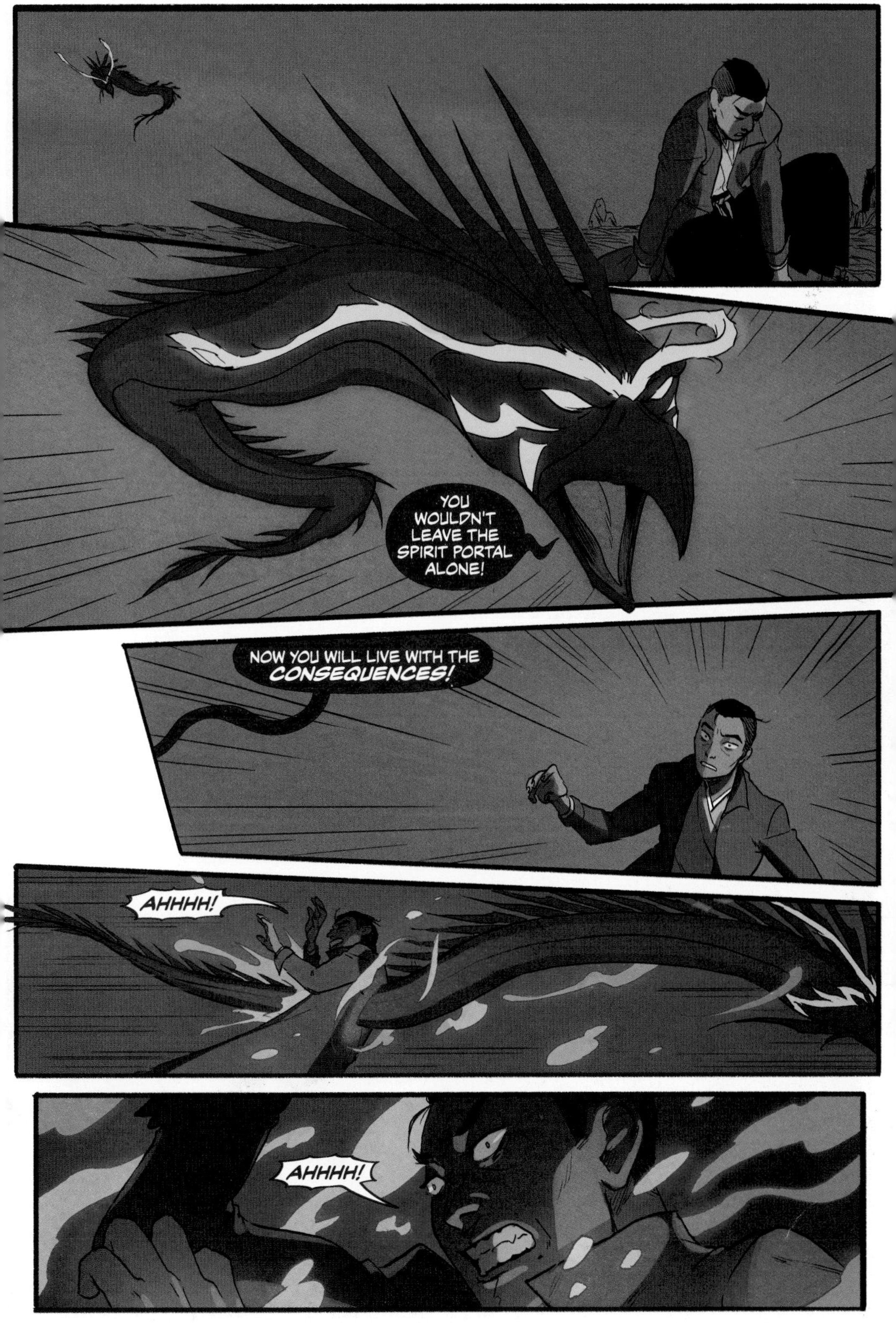
YOU WOULDN'T LEAVE THE SPIRIT PORTAL ALONE!
NOW YOU WILL LIVE WITH THE CONSEQUENCES!
AHHHH!
AHHHH!

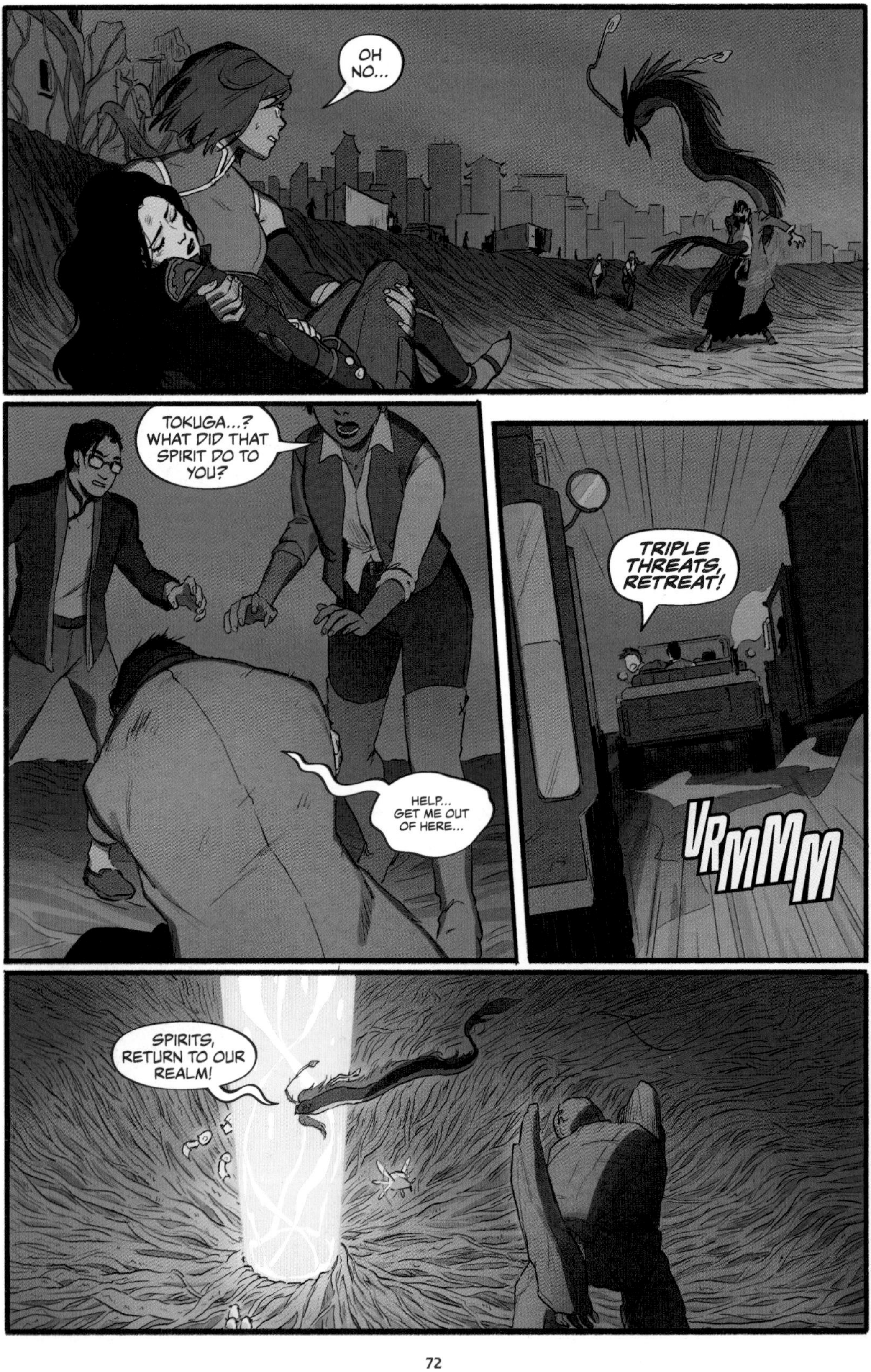
OH NO...
TOKUGA...? WHAT DID THAT SPIRIT DO TO YOU?
HELP... GET ME OUT OF HERE...
TRIPLE THREATS, RETREAT!
VRMMMM
SPIRITS, RETURN TO OUR REALM!

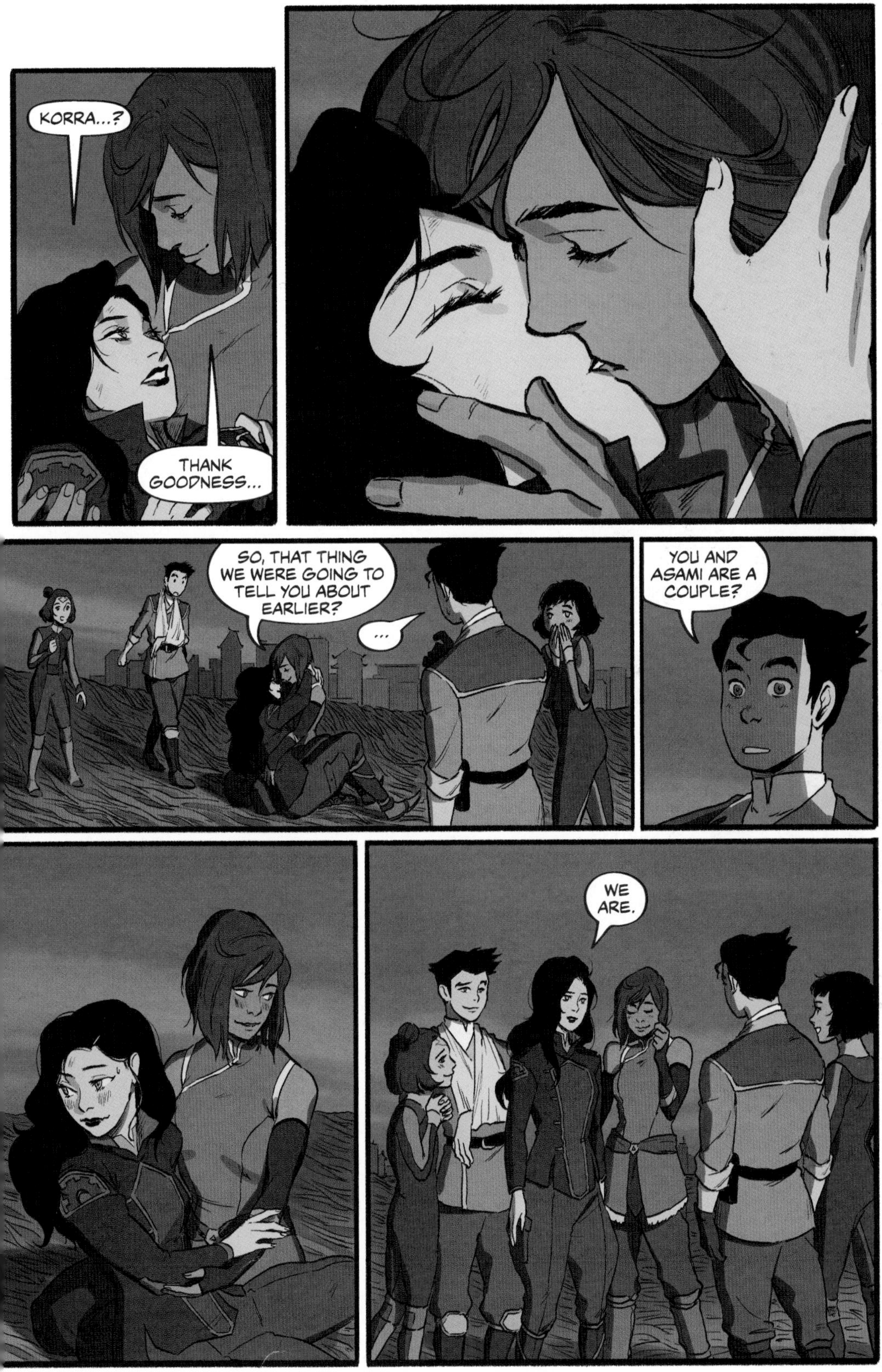
KORRA...?
THANK GOODNESS...
SO, THAT THING WE WERE GOING TO TELL YOU ABOUT EARLIER?
...
YOU AND ASAMI ARE A COUPLE?
WE ARE.

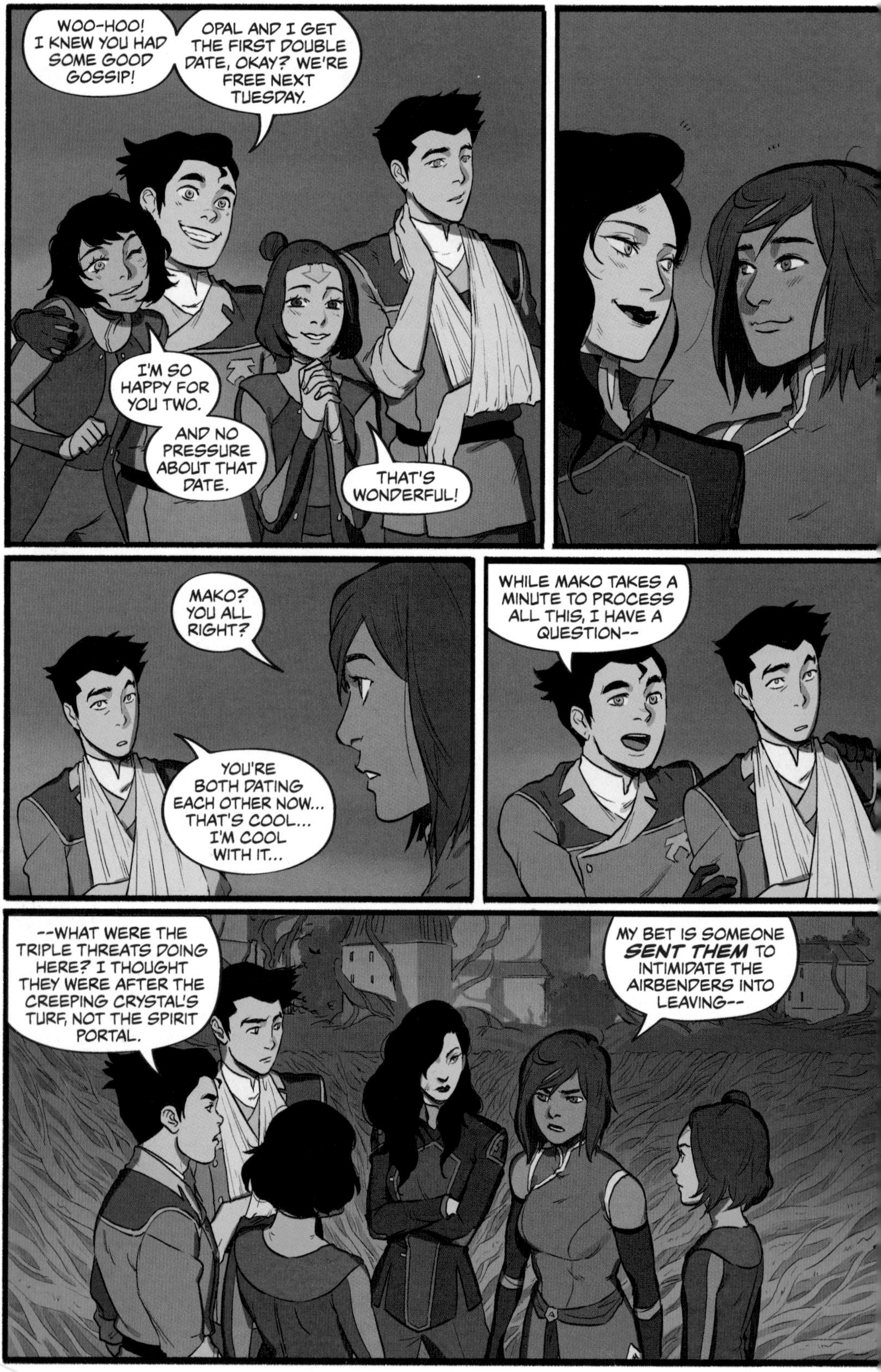
WOO-HOO! I KNEW YOU HAD SOME GOOD GOSSIP!
OPAL AND I GET THE FIRST DOUBLE DATE, OKAY? WE'RE FREE NEXT TUESDAY.
I'M SO HAPPY FOR YOU TWO.
AND NO PRESSURE ABOUT THAT DATE.
THAT'S WONDERFUL!
MAKO? YOU ALL RIGHT?
YOU'RE BOTH DATING EACH OTHER NOW... THAT'S COOL... I'M COOL WITH IT...
WHILE MAKO TAKES A MINUTE TO PROCESS ALL THIS, I HAVE A QUESTION--
--WHAT WERE THE TRIPLE THREATS DOING HERE? I THOUGHT THEY WERE AFTER THE CREEPING CRYSTAL'S TURF, NOT THE SPIRIT PORTAL.
MY BET IS SOMEONE **SENT THEM** TO INTIMIDATE THE AIRBENDERS INTO LEAVING--

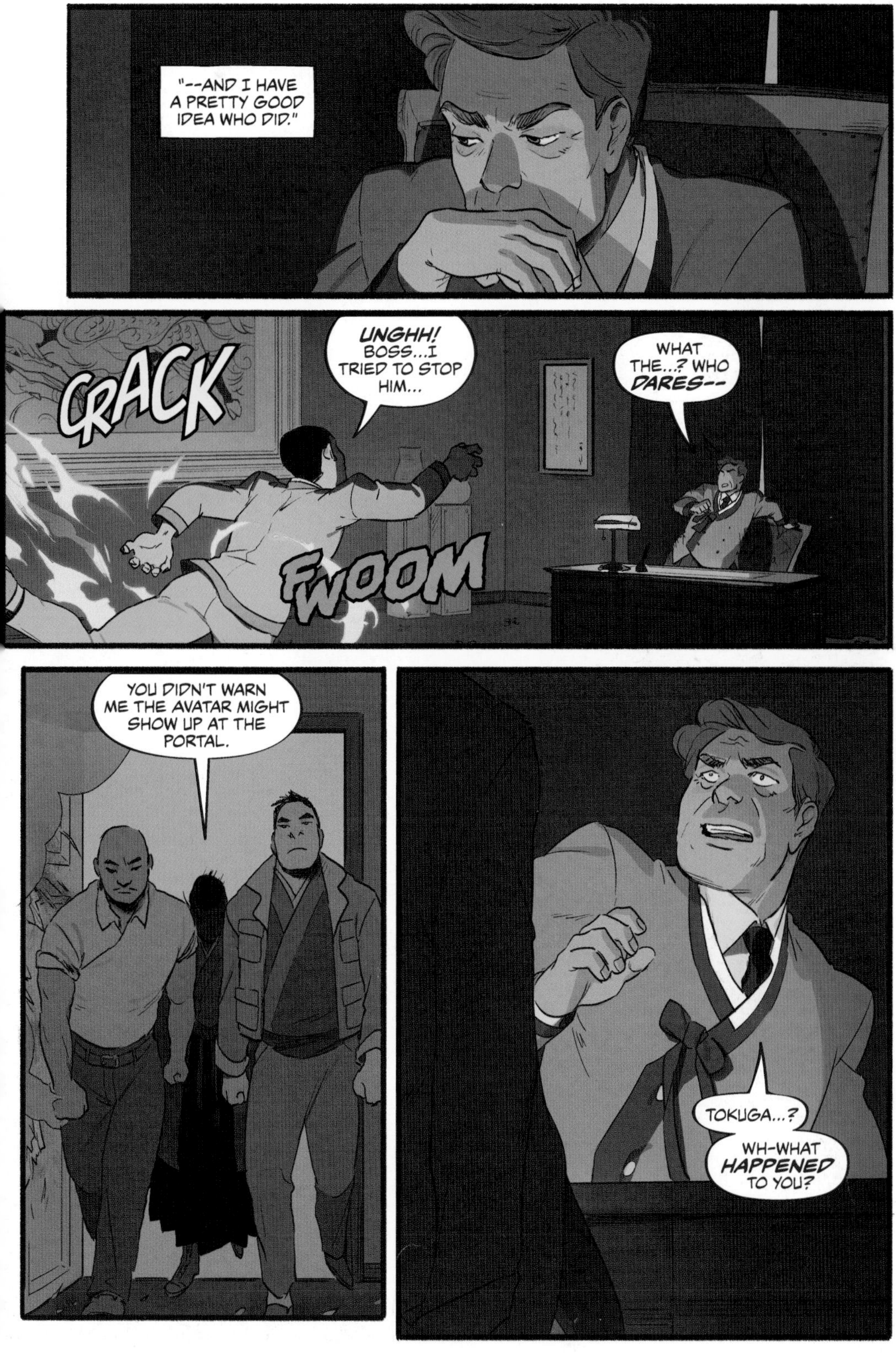
"--AND I HAVE A PRETTY GOOD IDEA WHO DID."
CRACK
UNGHH! BOSS...I TRIED TO STOP HIM...
WHAT THE...? WHO DARES--
FWOOM
YOU DIDN'T WARN ME THE AVATAR MIGHT SHOW UP AT THE PORTAL.
TOKUGA...?
WH-WHAT HAPPENED TO YOU?

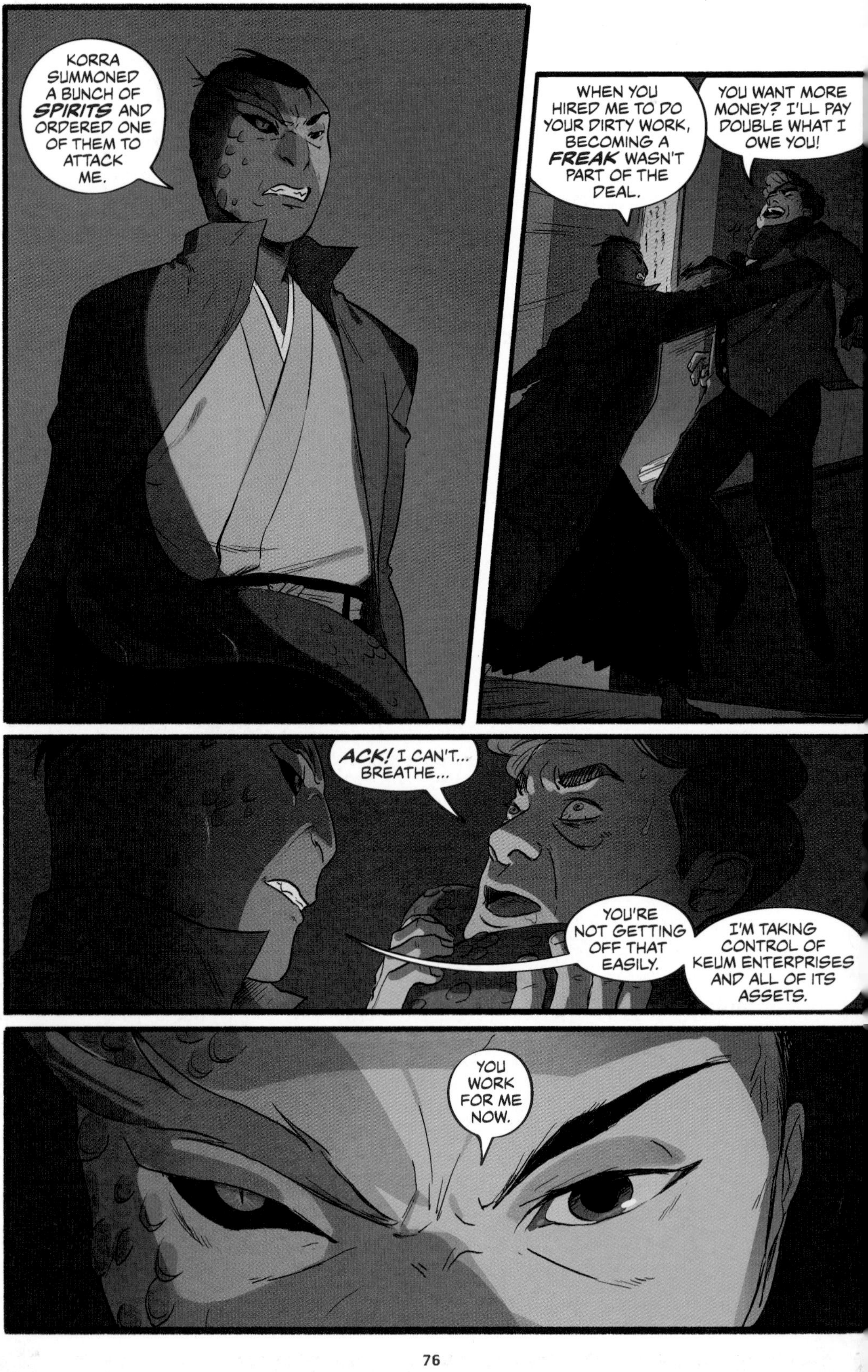
KORRA SUMMONED A BUNCH OF SPIRITS AND ORDERED ONE OF THEM TO ATTACK ME.
WHEN YOU HIRED ME TO DO YOUR DIRTY WORK, BECOMING A FREAK WASN'T PART OF THE DEAL.
YOU WANT MORE MONEY? I'LL PAY DOUBLE WHAT I OWE YOU!
ACK! I CAN'T... BREATHE...
YOU'RE NOT GETTING OFF THAT EASILY.
I'M TAKING CONTROL OF KEUM ENTERPRISES AND ALL OF ITS ASSETS.
YOU WORK FOR ME NOW.

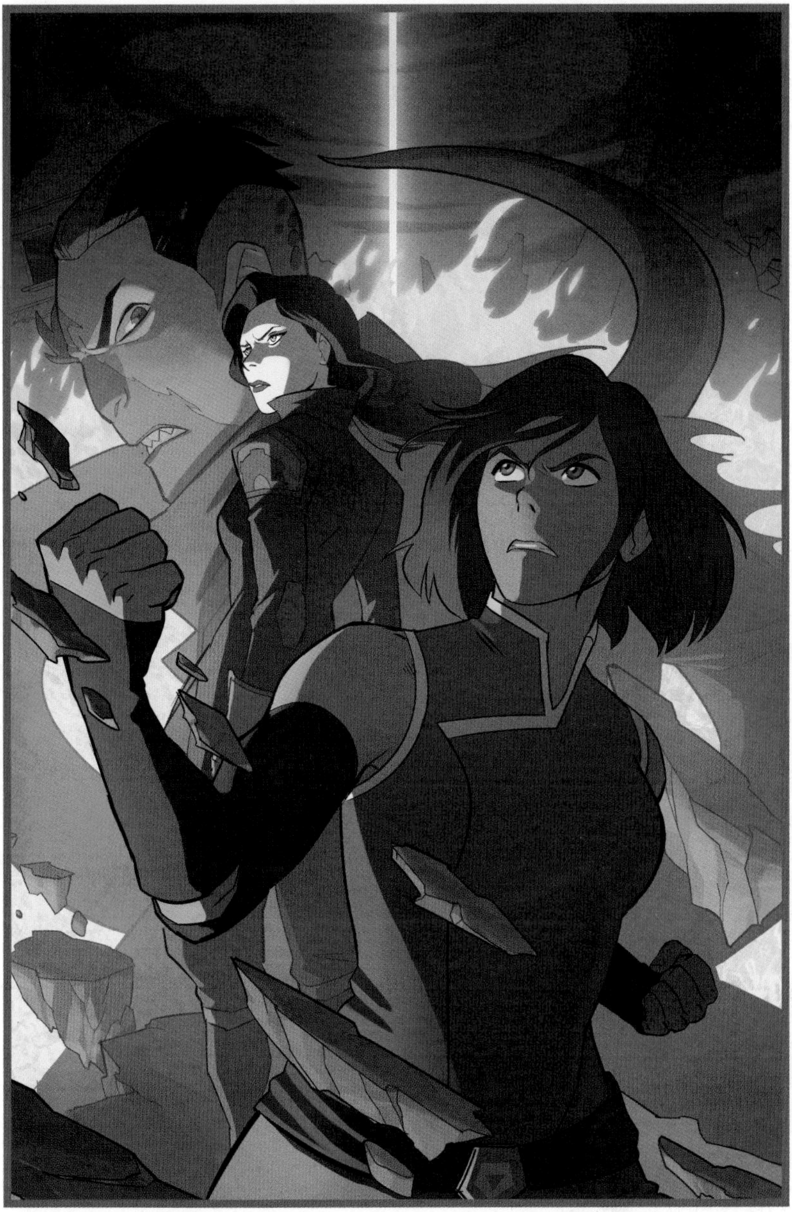

COMING IN JANUARY 2018!

Tokuga seeks revenge in . . .

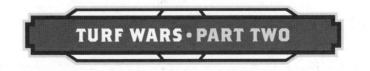

TURF WARS • PART TWO

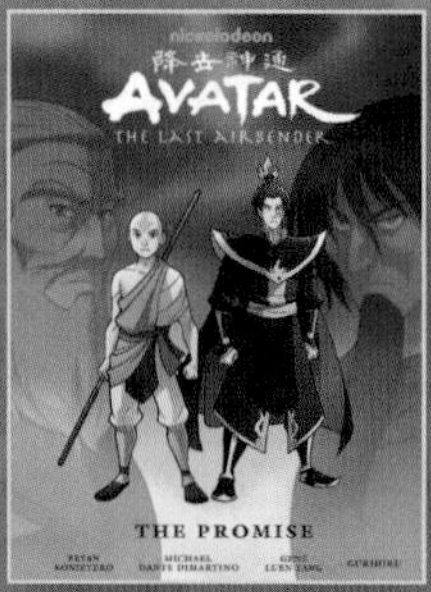
nickelodeon
AVATAR
THE LAST AIRBENDER
THE PROMISE

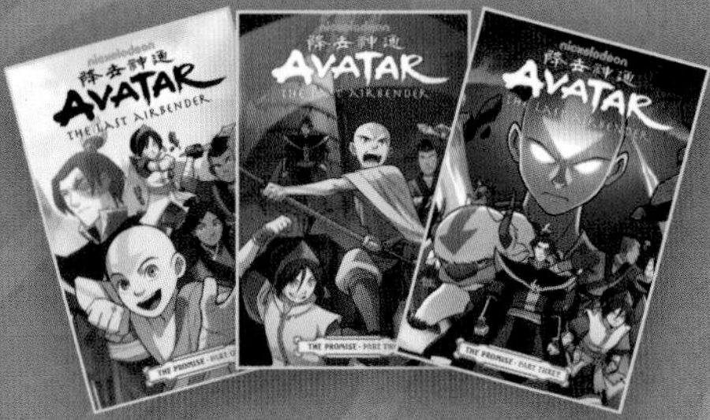
AVATAR
THE LAST AIRBENDER

Avatar: The Last Airbender—The Promise Library Edition
978-1-61655-074-5 $39.99

Avatar: The Last Airbender—The Promise Part 1
978-1-59582-811-8 $12.99

Avatar: The Last Airbender—The Promise Part 2
978-1-59582-875-0 $12.99

Avatar: The Last Airbender—The Promise Part 3
978-1-59582-941-2 $12.99

Avatar: The Last Airbender—The Search Library Edition
978-1-61655-226-8 $39.99

Avatar: The Last Airbender—The Search Part 1
978-1-61655-054-7 $12.99

Avatar: The Last Airbender—The Search Part 2
978-1-61655-190-2 $12.99

Avatar: The Last Airbender—The Search Part 3
978-1-61655-184-1 $12.99

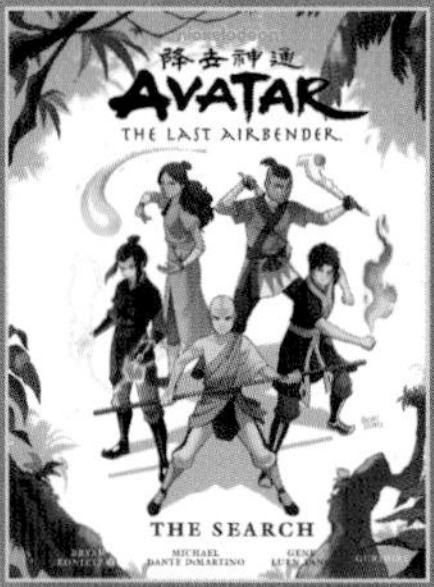
AVATAR
THE LAST AIRBENDER
THE SEARCH

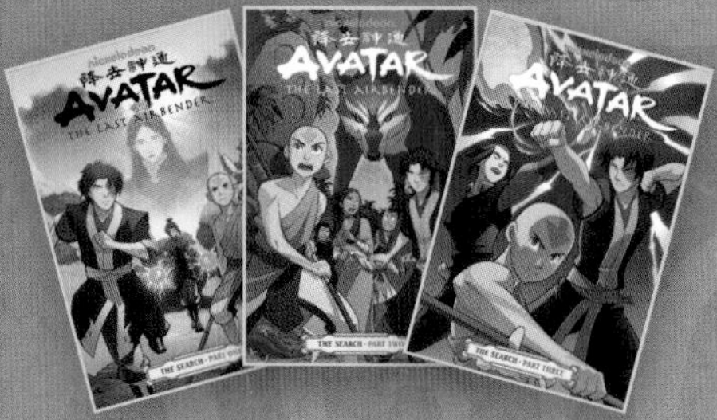
AVATAR
THE LAST AIRBENDER

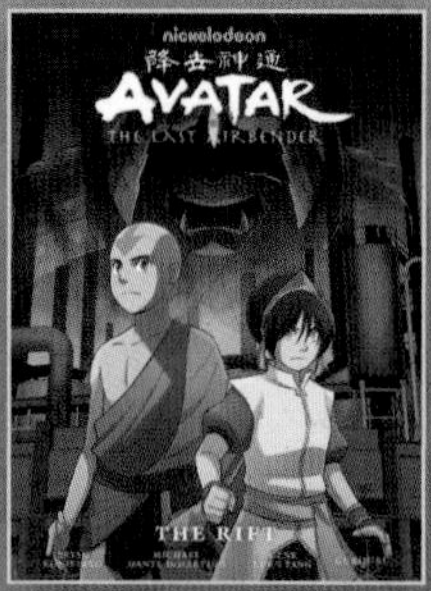
nickelodeon
AVATAR
THE LAST AIRBENDER

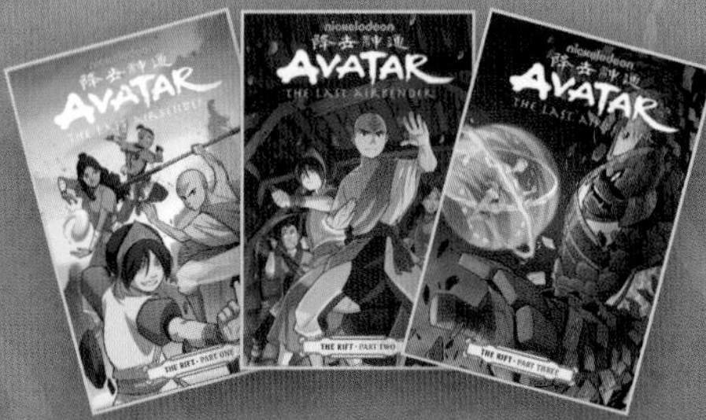
AVATAR

Avatar: The Last Airbender—The Rift Library Edition
978-1-61655-550-4 $39.99

Avatar: The Last Airbender—The Rift Part 1
978-1-61655-295-4 $12.99

Avatar: The Last Airbender—The Rift Part 2
978-1-61655-296-1 $12.99

Avatar: The Last Airbender—The Rift Part 3
978-1-61655-297-8 $12.99

Avatar: The Last Airbender—Smoke and Shadow Library Edition
978-1-50670-013-7 $39.99

Avatar: The Last Airbender—Smoke and Shadow Part 1
978-1-61655-761-4 $12.99

Avatar: The Last Airbender—Smoke and Shadow Part 2
978-1-61655-790-4 $12.99

Avatar: The Last Airbender—Smoke and Shadow Part 3
978-1-61655-838-3 $12.99

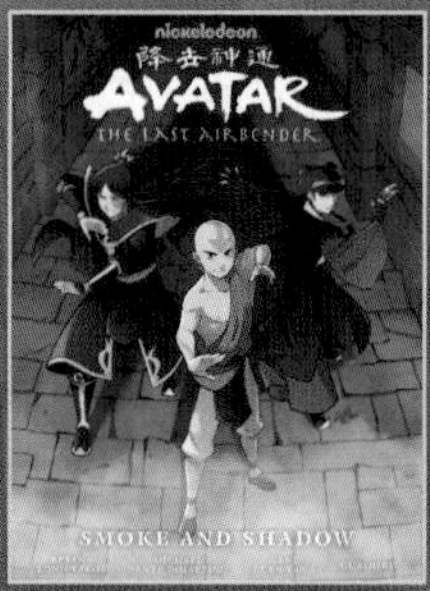
nickelodeon
AVATAR
THE LAST AIRBENDER
SMOKE AND SHADOW

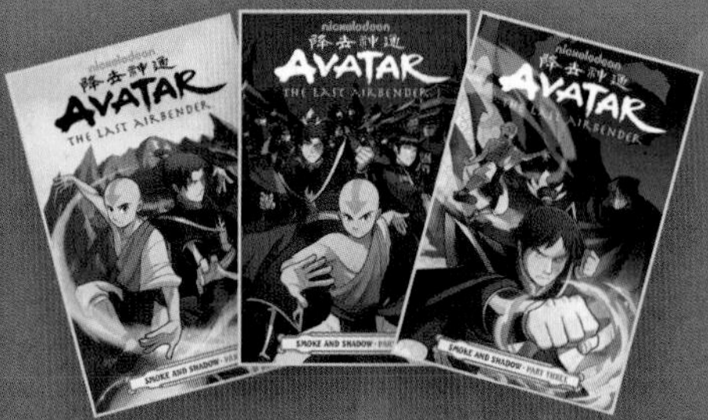
AVATAR
THE LAST AIRBENDER